D1195082

# POETRY ROCKS!

# World Poetry

## "Evidence of Life"

Paula Johanson

E | **Enslow Publishers, Inc.**
40 Industrial Road
Box 398
Berkeley Heights, NJ 07922
USA
http://www.enslow.com

For my teachers—"Seek not to question other than
the books I leave behind."

*"Poetry is just the evidence of life.*
*If your life is burning well, poetry is just the ash."*

—Leonard Cohen

Copyright © 2010 by Paula Johanson

**Library of Congress Cataloging-in-Publication Data**

Johanson, Paula.
    World poetry, "evidence of life" / Paula Johanson.
        p. cm. — (Poetry rocks!)
    Includes bibliographical references and index.
    Summary: "Discover some of the poetry of famed world poets, including: Sin-leqi-unninni,
Vyasa, Homer, Du Fu, Omar Khayyam, Rumi, Dante, Basho, Shevchenko, Tagore, Ahkmatova,
Lorca, Neruda, Walcott, and Cohen"—Provided by publisher.
        ISBN 978-0-7660-3280-4
        1. Poetry—History and criticism—Juvenile literature. 2. Poets—Biography—Juvenile
literature. 3. Poetry—Collections—Juvenile literature. 4. Poetry—Translations into English—
Juvenile literature. I. Title.
        PN1111.J65 2010
        809.1—dc22                                   2009044156

Printed in the United States of America

122009 Lake Book Manufacturing, Inc., Melrose Park, IL

10 9 8 7 6 5 4 3 2 1

**To Our Readers:** We have done our best to make sure all Internet addresses in this book were active
and appropriate when we went to press. However, the author and the publisher have no control over
and assume no liability for the material available on those Internet sites or on other Web sites they
may link to. Any comments or suggestions can be sent by e-mail to comments@enslow.com or to the
address on the back cover.

We have made every effort to locate all copyright holders of material used in this book. If any omissions
or errors have occurred, corrections will be made in future editions.

♻ Enslow Publishers, Inc., is committed to printing our books on recycled paper. The paper in every
book contains 10% to 30% postconsumer waste (PCW). The cover board on the outside of each book
contains 100% PCW. Our goal is to do our part to help young people and the environment too!

**Illustration Credits:** Art Archive/Alfredo Dagli Orti, p. 56; Associated Press, pp. 81, 130; Everett,
pp. 12, 110, 120, 141; Granger Collection, pp. 39, 101; Photos.com, pp. 22, 31, 63, 91; Private
Collection/The Bridgeman Art Library, p. 49; Shutterstock, pp. 1, 5, 11, 21, 30, 38, 48, 55, 62, 71,
80, 90, 100, 109, 119, 129, 140; Wikimedia Commons, p. 72.

**Cover Illustration:** Shutterstock

# Contents

## Permissions

Excerpt from "Gilgamesh: Beginnings" from *Gilgamesh: The Play*, translated by Derrek Hines. Copyright © Oberon Books Ltd.

Excerpt from "Divani Shamsi Tabriz" by Rumi, translated by Maryam Mafi, copyright © HarperCollins Publishers Ltd © 2002. Excerpts from "A Sleep and a Forgetting" and "And Patience Flees My Heart" from *Love: The Joy That Wounds* by Rumi, translated by Nahal Tajadad and Elfreda Powell. Copyright © Souvenir Press.

"Ditty of First Desire," "Sonnet of the Sweet Complaint," and "The Gypsy and the Wind" by Federico García Lorca, translated by Robert Pring-Mill. Copyright © HarperCollins Publishers Ltd.

Pablo Neruda's "Love Sonnet XVII," from *Still Another Day* (2005), is translated by William O'Daly and used by permission of Copper Canyon Press, www.coppercanyonpress.org. "The White Man's Burden (VI)" from *100 Love Sonnets* (1986), is translated by Stephen Tapscott, copyright © University of Texas Press.

"Crusoe's Island" and "Codicil" by Derek Walcott, copyright © by Farrar, Straus and Giroux.

"Suzanne" by Leonard Cohen, copyright 1967 Sony/ATV Music Publishing LLC. All rights administered by Sony/ATV Music Publishing LLC, 8 Music Square West, Nashville, TN 37203. All rights reserved. Used by permission. "Famous Blue Raincoat" by Leonard Cohen, copyright 1971 Sony/ATV Music Publishing LLC. All rights administered by Sony/ATV Music Publishing LLC, 8 Music Square West, Nashville, TN 37203. All rights reserved. Used by permission. "Closing Time" by Leonard Cohen, copyright 1992 Sony/ATV Music Publishing LLC. All rights administered by Sony/ATV Music Publishing LLC, 8 Music Square West, Nashville, TN 37203. All rights reserved. Used by permission.

We have made every effort to locate all copyright holders of material used in this book. If any omissions or errors have occurred, corrections will be made in future editions.

# INTRODUCTION

**P**oetry has special purposes. "In the history of human culture there is no example of a conscious adjustment of the various factors of personal and social life to new extensions except in the puny and peripheral efforts of artists," wrote Marshall McLuhan.[1] The artists who use carefully chosen words, in their efforts to be conscious of the factors of personal and social life in their cultures, are poets.

Words are used in many ways and for many purposes, but poetry has always been a special use of language. We can all learn to count objects and make lists, we can ask someone to do something or write a letter, we can talk about plans or keep business records—but poetry is special and different from all those uses of words. Whether spoken aloud or written down, poetry uses words in significant ways, different from a casual conversation.

Poets use words to impress the listeners with a shared experience. Because of this experience connecting us to each other, to our shared past and the world around us, poems are deeply meaningful in a personal sense as well as a cultural sense. Even people who say they do not like or understand poetry know the importance of singing a national anthem or making wedding vows, using formal words.

Poetry chanted aloud was an important part of many cultures, both before and after written records became common. Some oral poetry was and is composed spontaneously. Some was and is intended for a single occasion, not composed with the intent that it be permanently recorded. Ursula K. Le Guin calls these "butterfly poems—you can't make them stay."[2] Some modern oral poetry forums, such as poetry slams and rap, are spreading through urban centers of Western nations, as people from many modern cultures are rediscovering the enjoyable and powerful communication of poetry spoken aloud, as it has been enjoyed since the Stone Age.

In the twenty-first century, many people around the world have newspapers, radio, and television for sharing the news, and libraries full of magazines and books about recent and past events. We talk with each other over long distances by telephone and the Internet, and many of us travel to distant places, too. Life was not always like that for most people (and sadly, life is still not like that for most people in many nations). Until the modern era, only a few people traveled from place to place. Books, letters, and the news were rare treasures. It was a daring adventure to make a journey of five hundred miles. Instead of books and modern media, in many places people relied on the oral memory of a poet.

Some oral poets were informal and self-appointed, while others were highly trained by a master or group of masters to memorize and create poetry according to a formal tradition. In Greece in the eighth, seventh, and sixth centuries B.C.E., professional oral poets called *aoidoi* would orally compose and sing epic poems. An aoidos would use repeated, standard descriptions to aid his memory and make remembering or creating lines easier. Among the Anglo-Saxons, a scop also had some of the functions of a modern journalist, as would a skald for the Scandinavians, while for the

Celtic peoples, a bard provided many of the services we see today from barristers and judges as well. In the West African countries, such as Mali and Gambia, *griots* and *jeli* are still relied upon by their communities to recite family histories and genealogy and to compose topical commentaries. Around the world, poets have always been called on by their communities to recite poems about past events and invent new poems about new events. Sometimes a poet would be supported by a community for a year or many years, but some poets traveled from place to place bringing new stories. Around the world since ancient times, recognized poets of great talent have always been held in high esteem in their cultures, much like a rock star on tour or a circuit court judge.

Most of the poets discussed here are men. Around the world, women certainly did and do make and write and recite poetry, from lullabies to popular songs and even formal verse. But in some cultures, and in the past, women did not usually receive as much formal education as men, and women's use of poetry was more likely to be in their homes, whether a humble cottage or a fine manor or in the seclusion of a nunnery. In the past and in some cultures, poetry that was performed or published and distributed for a wide audience was usually by men. It is still the

## FACTS

### Dating Methods

You are probably familiar with the terms B.C. (before Christ) and A.D. (*anno Domini*, "in the year of the Lord") to indicate dates. The abbreviations B.C.E. (before the common era) and C.E. (common era) mean the same thing as B.C. and A.D. They are more often used by scholars and will be used in this book.

In addition, this book uses the abbreviation "c." to indicate approximate dates. It is short for the Latin term *circa*, meaning "around."

belief of some cultures that women should not display their creations and themselves publicly in that way. Of course, no one will ever know how many male poets presented the work of their wives or sisters as if it were their own.

Most of the poets discussed here spoke or speak Indo-European languages (languages of India and Europe, descended from Sanskrit). Around the world, people of all cultures did and do make and recite poetry of many kinds. Some of this poetry is being translated into Indo-European languages for publication and distribution in world markets still dominated by the lasting effects of colonialism and cultural imperialism. There are publishers, in Canada and other countries, making particular efforts to facilitate publication of literature in many mother tongues, not only English, French, and Spanish. But in a brief, introductory book such as this one, only a few poets of great influence are being profiled. Though this book does not focus on poets from among the aboriginal nations of the Americas, or from among the Australian aborigines and the peoples of the Pacific Islands, or living in Africa, it is important to acknowledge here that poets of great talent were and are present in all these places, and recognition of that talent is emerging outside their own cultures.

The publishing of written verses made it much easier for many poems to be preserved till the present day, usually with the poet's name recorded as well. But the invention of writing meant only that poetry could be preserved, not that what survived in spite of fire, flood, and decay was necessarily the best that could be created by that author or culture. All that remains of Anglo-Saxon literature, for example, are four books; if from this sampling the epic poem *Beowulf* has had such an inspiring effect on English literature and the arts, one wonders what other legacies were lost, not merely in Anglo-Saxon but around the world in many languages. The epic of *Gilgamesh* was only rediscovered in 1872 (preserved, paradoxically, because of a fire in ancient times that baked many clay tablets in the ruins of King Ashurbanipal's library). It is certain that there were and still are international poets in many languages who are worthy peers of Homer and Dante whose works have been lost to history, in part at least because the resources necessary to distribute published works were prohibitively expensive until the twentieth century.

# FACTS

## Poetic Meter and Rhyme

The meter of a verse is measured by the number of stressed syllables in a line. Each unit of syllables within a line is called a foot, which has one stressed syllable (marked with a /) and three, two, one, or no unstressed syllables (marked with a ∪). Line lengths are labeled as follows:

> one foot: monometer
> two feet: dimeter
> three feet: trimeter
> four feet: tetrameter
> five feet: pentameter

Lines of six or seven feet (hexameter or heptameter) are seen in other languages, such as French or Greek, but do not sound harmonious in English.

There are several common patterns for a metrical foot:

> iambic  (∪ /) ("When in disgrace with fortune and men's eyes")
> trochaic (/ ∪)  ("Mary had a little lamb")
> dactylic (/ ∪ ∪)  ("Listen, my children, and you shall hear")
> anapestic  (∪ ∪ /) ("'Twas the night before Christmas")
> spondee (/ / )  ("top gun"; "ice cream")

Rhyme schemes are identified by assigning a letter of the alphabet to each sound at the end of a line. For example, in the nursery rhyme "Humpty Dumpty," lines one and two (ending with "wall" and "fall") rhyme, so both of those lines are assigned the letter a. The next two lines end with "men" and "again." They are assigned the letter b because they are different from a but similar to each other:

> Humpty Dumpty sat on a wall, (a)
> Humpty Dumpty had a great fall. (a)
> All the king's horses and all the king's men (b)
> Couldn't put Humpty together again. (b)

> Thus, the complete rhyme scheme is aabb.

With the development of modern paper production and copying machines, and because access to the Internet is available in many places around the world, publishing a work of poetry now can be as affordable as a meal. But affordable publishing alone is not enough unless there is also freedom of speech, so that poets and others may have public forums to speak their words aloud, and their works may be published online or in print format without fear of violent suppression. It is a wonderful, powerful thing for world literature that many poets and writers around the world enjoy affordable publishing opportunities as well as freedom of speech. The resulting flood of abundant poetry of varying merits can be a little daunting for the reader. Who could ever read it all? And who would ever want to read much of it?

But poems are like city buses. If you don't want this one, there'll be another one along in a few minutes. And that poem may be by another Lorca in the twenty-first century, before he, too, is taken out and shot without trial for presenting poetry to a public audience. It is not necessary to write anthems, as Tagore did, to become a figurehead or a target. And as Akhmatova learned, suppression and censorship affect nations and cultures, not just poets. Even with the new technologies extending our communications, we need our personal and social lives to have continued conscious adjustment, with the assistance of poets and other artists.

# 1

## Sin-Leqi-Unninni, the Gilgamesh Poet

### (c. 1200 B.C.E.)

Gilgamesh was king of the city of Uruk in Babylonia, around the year 2800 B.C.E. His name was recorded in lists of the kings of Sumer ruling after the Flood, in southern Mesopotamia, on the river Euphrates in what is now Iraq. The *Epic of Gilgamesh* was composed nearly five thousand years ago, as a king's memoir that grew together with the retelling of ancient myths and folklore into one complete work.

The version of the poem that is most complete was composed about 1200 B.C.E. by a scholar-priest named Sin-leqi-unninni, the first author whose name is recorded in history. Nothing more is known about this poet. In the ruins of Nineveh, near the modern city of Mosul, twelve incomplete clay tablets were found in 1853, among the library collection of King Ashurbanipal. These tablets, copies made about the seventh century B.C.E.,

A relief image of Gilgamesh was carved in the ninth century B.C.E. in Assyria.

tell the story of Gilgamesh, written in the Akkadian language using cuneiform writing.

This version is based on an Old Babylonian version found later, written about 1700 B.C.E., of which eleven fragments survive, including three nearly complete tablets. Fragments of the *Gilgamesh* epic were found later in several places in Mesopotamia, Syria, and Turkey. Also, five shorter poems about Gilgamesh have been discovered, written in Sumerian about 2100 B.C.E. Textual information from these poems has been used to fill in many of the gaps from the Nineveh tablets, so that nearly two thousand lines of the original three thousand lines of text are readable, with gaps in the surviving text.

The story of King Gilgamesh and his friend Enkidu builds on ancient myths and has shaped storytelling for nearly five thousand years. Gilgamesh has become an arrogant tyrant of Uruk, and Enkidu is created as an innocent savage, to be a match for him. After Enkidu is "civilized through the erotic arts of a temple priestess," as Stephen Mitchell writes, they become heartfelt friends. "With him Gilgamesh battles monsters, and when Enkidu dies, he is inconsolable. He sets out on a desperate journey to find the one man who can tell him how to escape death."[1] During his search, Gilgamesh is told of the Great Flood, copied from a story written a thousand years earlier in the Atrahasis.

## Summary and Explication

This is an introduction to a great hero, telling of his travels, the city he built, and the record he left, saying in grand terms: "Been there, done that, sent the postcards."

### Prologue

*He had seen everything, had experienced all emotions,
from exaltation to despair, had been granted a vision
into the great mystery, the secret places,
the primeval days before the Flood. He had journeyed
to the edge of the world and made his way back, exhausted
but whole. He had carved his trials on stone tablets,
had restored the holy Eanna Temple and the massive
wall of Uruk, which no city on earth can equal.
See how its ramparts gleam like copper in the sun.
Climb the stone staircase, more ancient than the mind
        can imagine,
approach the Eanna Temple, sacred to Ishtar,
a temple that no king has equaled in size or beauty,
walk on the wall of Uruk, follow its course
around the city, inspect its mighty foundations,
examine its brickwork, how masterfully it is built,
observe the land it encloses: the palm trees, the gardens,
the orchards, the glorious palaces and temples, the shops
and marketplaces, the houses, the public squares.
Find the cornerstone and under it the copper box
that is marked with his name. Unlock it. Open the lid.
Take out the tablet of lapis lazuli. Read
how Gilgamesh suffered all and accomplished all.*

## Poetic Techniques

In the original Akkadian verse, the poetry was composed with care for evocative imagery, short phrases easily spoken aloud, and repetitive phrasing. The translator chose a loose form of tetrameter lines, with four stressed syllables per line, except for the Prologue and the ending, which have five beats per line and seem to be the original work of Sin-leqi-unninni. Because the original was not Anglo-Saxon verse, the translator avoided English poetic devices such as alliteration and iambic rhythms, and he also took care that end rhymes and identical rhythms never appear in two consecutive lines.

## Themes

As another poet and translator noted, "The poem enthralled the ancient world as it does ours because it touches on the themes of our common humanity: love, death and friendship."[2] It also shows how even then, people were aware that living in a great city was different from farming and herding in small groups, and especially different from wandering alone in the wilderness.

The concept of hubris, the overweening pride that goes before a fall, which later became so important in Greek tragedy, was not yet developed. This is not a poem of failed pride, as in Shelley's "Ozymandias" with the line "Look on my works, ye mighty, and despair!" This epic is a story about telling the story of the greatest hero the world had known. The writer of this epic and the audience knew the facts well: Heroes are larger than life, beloved and punished by the gods, and they die like all humans. The author is saying to his audience, "This is how to tell the grand story. Participate in the process with me."

## Commentary

Mitchell read at least thirteen recent versions of the epic, as well as commentaries in English and German, and he prepared a rough prose version before beginning his real work of translating the epic into poetry in English. This was a proper and decent preparation by a working poet who is bilingual in English and German, though not Akkadian and Sumerian. Each poet who translates or paraphrases Gilgamesh makes, as Derrek Hines says, "an effort to recapture for the modern reader some of the vigour and excitement the original audience must have felt."[3]

The six-mile-long wall around Uruk has been excavated and investigated; it enclosed a planned and harmonious city many times the size of any other until Rome was built. "Our ability to imagine the walls— our inability not to as we read the sentence that describes them—once again makes the act of narration part of the story and forces us, as readers, into the world of the text," wrote Arthur Brown.[4]

# FACTS

## Finding Gilgamesh

The story of Gilgamesh had been lost until George Smith, a young British Museum curator, began translating these twelve cuneiform records in 1872, from seventy-three fragments of at least three copies. He recognized the biblical story of the Great Flood when reading one fragment "in the form of a speech from the hero of the Deluge."[5] Overcome, he set the tablet on the table and rushed about the room in a great state of excitement. He began to undress himself, to the astonishment of his colleagues, in a moment that echoes Allan Ginsberg disrobing during readings of "Howl," Archimedes crying "Eureka!" and running naked from his bath, and the character Enkidu emerging naked from the wilderness.

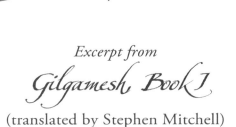

Excerpt from

# *Gilgamesh, Book I*

## (translated by Stephen Mitchell)

*(After the priestess Shamhat has showed him what a woman is, for seven days)*

*… Enkidu sat down at Shamhat's feet.*
*He looked at her, and he understood*
*all the words she was speaking to him.*
*"Now, Enkidu, you know what it is*
*to be with a woman, to unite with her.*
*You are beautiful, you are like a god.*
*Why should you roam the wilderness*
*and live like an animal? Let me take you*
*to great-walled Uruk, to the temple of Ishtar,*
*to the palace of Gilgamesh the mighty king,*
*who in his arrogance oppresses the people,*
*trampling upon them like a wild bull."*

*She finished, and Enkidu nodded his head.*
*Deep in his heart he felt something stir,*
*a longing he had never known before,*
*the longing for a true friend. Enkidu said,*
*"I will go, Shamhat. Take me with you*
*to great-walled Uruk, to the temple of Ishtar,*
*to the palace of Gilgamesh the mighty king.*
*I will challenge him. I will shout to his face*
*'I am the mightiest! I am the man*
*who can make the world tremble! I am supreme!'"*

*"Come," said Shamhat, "let us go to Uruk,*
*I will lead you to Gilgamesh the mighty king,*
*You will see the great city with its massive wall,*

*you will see the young men dressed in their splendor,*
*in the finest linen and embroidered wool,*
*brilliantly colored, with fringed shawls and wide*
*belts....*
*You who are still so ignorant of life,*
*I will show you Gilgamesh the mighty king,*
*the hero destined for both joy and grief.*
*You will stand before him and gaze with wonder,*
*you will see how handsome, how virile he is,*
*how his body pulses with erotic power.*
*He is even taller and stronger than you—*
*so full of life force that he needs no sleep.*
*Enkidu, put aside your aggression...."*

*Excerpt from*

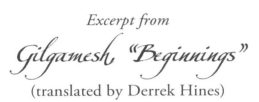

(translated by Derrek Hines)

*Here is Gilgamesh, king of Uruk:*
*two-thirds divine, a mummy's boy,*
*zeppelin ego, cock like a trip-hammer,*
*and solid chrome, no-prisoners arrogance.*

*Pulls women like beer rings.*
*Grunts when puzzled.*
*A bully. A jock. Perfecto. But in love?—*
*a moon-calf, and worse, thoughtful.*

*Next, a one-off:*
*clay and lightning entangled by the gods*
*to create a strong-man from the wastelands*
*to curb Gilgamesh—named Enkidu.*

*Sour electric fear, desert mirage at your throat,*
*strong enough to hold back the night,*
*so handsome he robs the world of horizon—*
*for no one's gaze lifts beyond him....*

## Critical Response To The Epic of Gilgamesh

"Here is the epic of the fear of death, arisen in the immemorial among people who were the first for whom the separation between life and death became definitive and fateful,"[6] Rainer Maria Rilke wrote to a friend. To another he said: "I ... consider it to be among the greatest things that can happen to a person."[7]

"But it also has a particular relevance in today's world, with its polarized fundamentalisms, each side fervently believing in its own righteousness, each on a crusade, or jihad, against what it perceives as an evil enemy," says Stephen Mitchell, introducing his controversial new translation. "The epic has an extraordinarily sophisticated moral intelligence. In its emphasis on balance and its refusal to side with either hero or monster, it leads us to question our dangerous certainties about good and evil."[8]

Andrew George's two-volume critical work is the most definitive standard edition of *Gilgamesh*, newly rereleased in 2003. Among the most ancient of literary works, this poem has such interest for modern readers that at least six new translations have been published since 2001.

"Have there been two such / as Gilgamesh and Enkidu / who released our first imagination / to map the new interior spaces we still / scribble on the backs of envelopes, of lives?" asked Derrek Hines in his 2002 interpretation of the epic. "They strode into deeds like furnaces / to flash off the husk of their humanity, / and emerged, purified of time."[9] These characters were the template for what constituted a "hero" in Western literature.

## Suggested Further Reading

This epic work influenced the *Mahabharata*, the writings of Homer, and the biblical stories of David and Jonathan, of *Job*, and *Ecclesiastes*, and through them nearly all of Indo-European literature and poetry. The mythic origins of the *Gilgamesh* story lie in the distant past before the ending of the last ice age and may even have connections to the traditional story of the Hamatsa from the Kwaguelth (formerly called Kwakiutl) aboriginal people from western Canada.

The influence of *Gilgamesh* lingers on in modern storytelling in the *Iron Hans* story from the Brothers Grimm, and through it *Iron John* by the poet Robert Bly and *Wild Man Island* by Will Hobbs. In Ursula K. Le Guin's book *The Wind's Twelve Quarters,* the poetic short story "The Ones Who Walk Away" tells of Omelas, a mythical city clearly influenced by Uruk. Also, Neal Stephenson's futuristic novel *Snow Crash* relies on references from *Gilgamesh.*

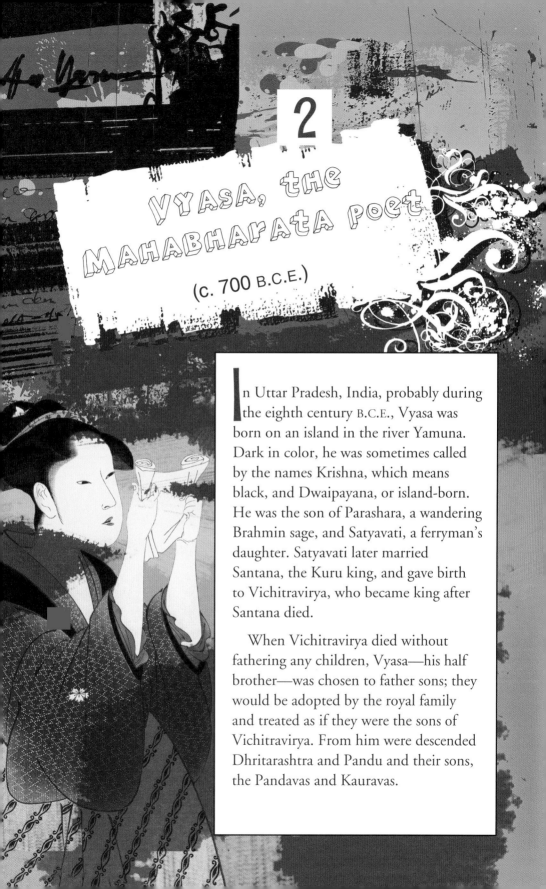

# 2

# VYASA, the MAHABHARATA POET

## (c. 700 B.C.E.)

In Uttar Pradesh, India, probably during the eighth century B.C.E., Vyasa was born on an island in the river Yamuna. Dark in color, he was sometimes called by the names Krishna, which means black, and Dwaipayana, or island-born. He was the son of Parashara, a wandering Brahmin sage, and Satyavati, a ferryman's daughter. Satyavati later married Santana, the Kuru king, and gave birth to Vichitravirya, who became king after Santana died.

When Vichitravirya died without fathering any children, Vyasa—his half brother—was chosen to father sons; they would be adopted by the royal family and treated as if they were the sons of Vichitravirya. From him were descended Dhritarashtra and Pandu and their sons, the Pandavas and Kauravas.

This painting from the British Museum shows a scene from
the *Mahabharata*: Arjuna in a carriage behind Krishna.

Because of this kinship, Vyasa was able to tell the history of the royal family, composing in Sanskrit the epic poem *Jaya*, in 8,800 verses. *Jaya* is structured as a dialogue between King Dhritarashtra and his adviser and chariot driver, Saniaya; it contains many details about each battle of the eighteen-day Kurukshetra War. Vyasa lived in a forest in Kurukshetra, very near the battlefield. Some scholars used to believe that *Jaya* was written in the twentieth century B.C.E. or earlier, but the war probably occurred in the eighth century B.C.E., making the epic much more recent.

This epic poem was to became the core of the *Mahabharata*, the great tale of the Bharata dynasty. Most scholars think that material was added to this great epic poem over a long period of time. In the sixth or fifth century B.C.E., the poem was expanded to twenty-four thousand verses in the *Bharata* as recited by Vaisampayana, and still later there were more than ninety thousand verses in the *Mahabharata* as recited by Ugrasravas.

There is no way to be certain how much of *Jaya* or the *Mahabharata* is authentic history and whether any of it was originally written as fiction, but this is a literary problem common to many ancient scriptural and devotional writings of any culture. Even Homer's *Iliad* used to be thought of as a work of pure fiction by many scholars until the discovery of the ruins of Troy. What is certain is that the *Mahabharata* is a work revered in its homeland, and that it has had lasting influence not only on the literature of India but on the scholars of other nations who visited India and became aware of this powerfully written epic poem.

Vyasa is also considered the author of the eighteen major Puranas of Hindu scripture, and his son Shuka is the narrator of the Bhagavata-Purana. Traditionally, Vyasa was supposed to have categorized the writings of the original single *Veda* into four parts, allowing people to understand the divine knowledge in it. *Vyasa* means to split, differentiate, or describe.

Excerpt from

# Book One, Adi Parva, Section One

(translated by Kisari Mohan Ganguli;
published 1883–1896)

*In this world, when it was destitute of brightness and light, and enveloped all around in total darkness, there came into being, as the primal cause of creation, a mighty egg, the one inexhaustible seed of all created beings. It is called Mahadivya, and was formed at the beginning of the Yuga, in which we are told, was the true light Brahma, the eternal one, the wonderful and inconceivable being present alike in all places; the invisible and subtile cause, whose nature partaketh of entity and non-entity. From this egg came out the lord Pitamaha Brama, the one only Prajapati; with Suraguru and Sthanu. Then appeared the twenty-one Prajapatis, viz., Manu, Vashsitha and Parameshthi; ten Prachetas, Daksha, and the seven sons of Daksha. Then appeared the man of inconceivable nature whom all the Rishis know and so the Viswe-devas, the Andityas, the Vasus, and the twin Aswins; the Yakshas, the Sadhyas, the Pisachas, the Guhyakas, and the Pitris. After these were produced the wise and most holy Brahmarshis, and the numerous Rajarshis distinguished by every noble quality. So the water, the heavens, the earth, the air, the sky, the points of the heavens, the years, the seasons, the months, the fortnights, called Pakshas, with day and night in due succession. And thus were produced all things which are known to mankind.*

*And what is seen in the universe, whether animate or inanimate, of created things, will at the end of the world, and after the expiration of the Yuga, be again confounded. And, at the commencement of other Yugas, all things will be renovated, and, like the various fruits of the earth, succeed each other in the due order of their seasons. Thus continueth perpetually to revolve in the world, without beginning and without end, this wheel which causeth the destruction of all things.*

**subtile**—subtle; elusive

**fortnights**—two-week periods

**confounded**—mixed together

## Summary and Explication

The creation of the world is described along with the origins of an extended family of heroic figures. All things in the world will be recombined at the end of the world and made into new things. New cycles of creation will proceed like the seasons of the year.

## Poetic Techniques

It is very easy to believe that these are teaching verses, composed to be recited aloud so that listeners may learn them by heart. The careful lists of the created things show reverence for both the natural world and for the creation of the great figures to people it. An air of mystery is maintained even after translation into English.

## Themes

This creation story has some elements in common with the creation story told in the first chapter of *Genesis* in the Old Testament of the Bible, part of the Hebrew Torah.

The "wheel which causeth the destruction of all things" is the same wheel that appears on a card of the Major Arcana in the deck of Tarot cards. It is an image as ancient as the fall of the Tower of Babel, which appears on another Tarot card. This revolving wheel that raises up and differentiates all created things then goes on to recycle and renovate them in a cycle of creation, destruction, and new creation. Appearances of this wheel can be found in the *Rubaiyat* of Omar Khayyam a thousand years later, and they continue in unbroken descent of literary imagery throughout Indo-European literature to the wheel's modern television appearance on the series *Wheel of Fortune*.

## Commentary

Some creation stories consciously try to be mysterious and cryptic, hinting that the teller knows more than she or he lets on. Others are composed to make the perspective they are trying to convey more understandable for the listener and reader. Vyasa took the second approach, even if the result is not at this point in time what a modern reader would often choose for casual light reading. Vyasa was a definer and the kind of writer who intended that his works be read and heard, considered, and held in one's heart. He did not, it appears, write merely for praise, though his name is celebrated among devout Hindus as Homer is among European scholars.

The tone at this point in the poem, during the creation story, is distinctly similar to the second chapter of Genesis and to Paul's First Letter to the Corinthians in the Bible. This is not only because all Indo-European cultures share some religious ancestry and influences as well as language roots, but also because modern English was shaped by the translation of the King James Bible into English, and because this translator of the *Mahabharata* was familiar with the King James Bible, as were all students of English literature at the end of the nineteenth century.

# FACTS

## Writing Down the *Mahabarata*

The first section of the *Mahabharata* states that as Vyasa recited from memory, Ganapati transcribed each stanza. But Ganapati could not keep up with the recitation and missed many words or even stanzas. Ganapati is both a name for the head of a republic from ancient India and an epithet for the elephant-headed Hindu deity Ganesha. The text includes a popular variation on the story of how Ganesha's right tusk was broken. His pen failed during the dictation, and he snapped off his tusk as a replacement.

The difficulty of writing down exactly what is being recited aloud has been faced by many transcribers. The reciter has memorized the entire composition and is not able to stop the dictation and resume it or repeat sections the scribe has missed.

*Excerpt from*

# Book One, Adi Parva, Section One

(translated by Kisari Mohan Ganguli;
published 1883–1896)

*Thou art acquainted, O prince, with the lenity and
severity of fate; this anxiety therefore for the safety of
thy children is unbecoming. Moreover, it behoveth
thee not to grieve for that which must happen: for
who can avert, by his wisdom, the decrees of fate?
No one can leave the way marked out for him by
Providence. Existence and non-existence, pleasure
and pain all have Time for their root. Time createth
all things and Time destroyeth all creatures. It is
Time that burneth creatures and it is Time that
extinguisheth the fire. All states, the good and the
evil, in the three worlds, are caused by Time. Time
cutteth short all things and createth them anew. Time
alone is awake when all things are asleep: indeed,
Time is incapable of being overcome. Time passeth
over all things without being retarded. Knowing,
as thou dost, that all things past and future and all
that exist at the present moment, are the offspring of
Time, it behoveth thee not to throw away thy reason.*

**lenity**—leniency; mercy

**behoveth**—is necessary or fit

**retarded**—slowed

## Critical Response To Vyasa

The original verses by Vyasa have been revered for nearly two thousand years as cultural history as well as devotional works and philosophy about the role of humanity in the universe. "The study of the Bharata is an act of piety. He that readeth even one foot, with belief, hath his sins entirely purged away," says the Introduction of Book One of the *Mahabharata*. "… as the sea is eminent among receptacles of water, and the cow among quadrupeds; … so is the Bharata said to be among histories."[1]

James Fitzgerald is among the scholars who consider the *Mahabharata* to be one of the two most important cultural works of India. "The *Mahabharata* and *Ramayana* still exert tremendous cultural influence throughout India and Southeast Asia," he says. "It presents sweeping visions of the cosmos and humanity and intriguing and frightening glimpses of divinity in an ancient narrative that is accessible, interesting, and compelling for anyone willing to learn the basic themes of India's culture."[2]

## Suggested Further Reading

Another great poetic work of Indian heritage is the *Ramayana*, composed by Valmiki in Sanskrit about the fourth century B.C.E. Early scholars believed it was written about 1500 B.C.E. A shortened, modern prose version of this epic poem was written by R. K. Narayan. More recent writers from India include Ghalib and Chatterjee.

Reading the scriptures and holy books of many cultures is a worthy study in comparative religious studies; it also gives insight into the secular cultures and improves the reader's understanding of common human perceptions and intentions. Most cultures have creation myths and great works about historical figures, which may be told in prose or poetry, and which have been translated into English.

# 3

# Homer

## (c. 700–600 B.C.E.)

The life of Homer is a mystery, with no details known. Two epic poems from ancient Greece, the *Iliad* and the *Odyssey,* are attributed to him, as are several hymns to the gods. He was an aoidos, or singer, the term used for a poet skilled in the oral composition and performance of epic poetry. He was traditionally believed to be blind.

From his works, scholars guess that he was an Attic Greek who may have been born in Turkey at Colophon or the seaport Smyrna, but other guesses for his birthplace include the island of Khios or the island of Rhodes in the Aegean Sea, in Cyprus at Salamis, or in Athens on the Greek mainland. It is not possible to be certain that he was the sole author of the works he is considered to have composed orally. After his death, other aoidoi recited his works as they traveled and at annual festivals in Athens.

A bust of the poet Homer

Classical Greek sources suggest that Homer lived long before the epic poems attributed to him were recorded in writing. The eighth century B.C.E. used to be considered by most literary authorities to be the time of Homer, but since about 1990 that belief has changed, and now the seventh century B.C.E. is thought by some scholars to be more likely.

As many epic poets did, Homer presented his narrative impersonally, only rarely drawing attention to himself, as in the first line of the *Iliad* when he addresses the goddess Calliope, who is the Muse of epic poetry. Poets believed they were inspired by the Muses and that the Muses could take away what inspiration they had given.

# FACTS

## The Greek Alphabet

There is a controversial theory that the Greek alphabet was invented about 800 B.C.E. by Palamedes, a Greek aristocrat, who adapted and modified the West Semitic syllabary. Barry B. Powell suggests that this was done not only to make it possible to write more than inventories and tax records in the Greek language, but for the particular purpose of being able to make a formal record of the poems of Homer.

*Excerpt from The Iliad, Book 19, lines 344–368*

# Briseis' lament for Patroclus

(translated by Ian Johnston)

*Briseis, looking like golden Aphrodite,*
*then saw Patroclus mutilated by sharp bronze.*
*With a cry, she threw herself on him, hands tearing*
*at her breast, her tender neck, her lovely face,*
*fair as a goddess, lamenting:*

> *"Patroclus,*
> *you who brought the utmost joy to my sad heart,*
> *I left you here alive, when I went off*
> *taken from these huts. But now, at my return,*
> *I find you dead, you, the people's leader.*
> *Again for me, as always, evil follows evil.*
>
> *I saw the husband I was given to*
> *by my father and my noble mother killed*
> *by sharp bronze before our city. My brothers,*
> *three of them, who my own mother bore,*
> *whom I loved, have all met their fatal day.*
> *But when swift Achilles killed my husband,*
> *you wouldn't let me weep. You told me then*
> *you'd make me lord Achilles' wedded wife,*
> *he'd take me in his ships to Phthia,*
> *for a marriage feast among the Myrmidons.*
> *You were always gentle. That's the reason*
> *I'll never stop this grieving for your death."*

*As Briseis said this, she wept. The women joined her*
*in wailing for Patroclus, though each of them*
*had her own private sorrows....*

## Summary and Explication

During the Trojan War, Briseis was a widowed queen of a city taken captive by Achilles, who became her lover. She was taken from Achilles by King Agamemnon to replace Agamemnon's captive Chryseis when she was returned to her people to avert a plague from Apollo and to punish Achilles for saying it was wrong for the king to take the lion's share of the war prizes. Achilles surrendered Briseis to Agamemnon but refused to fight anymore alongside the Greeks. His friend Patroclus fought instead and died. Achilles resolved to fight again, and Briseis was returned to his hut. There she found Patroclus "lying dead; and tearing her breast, neck, and cheeks, she mourned him who had always been so gentle towards her, and had never let her weep."[1]

## Poetic Techniques

This is only a short sample of 24 lines. In the entire poem there are 15,693 lines, which later Greek commentators divided into 24 books or scrolls.

In the original Greek, the lines are written in dactylic hexameter. In this pattern, there are six stressed syllables in each line, and each stressed syllable is followed by two unstressed syllables. From line to line, there may be some variations of stressed and unstressed syllables. Most modern translations of Homer's work into English are not in hexameter but instead are in prose, blank verse, or free-form poetry with four or five stressed syllables per line. A pattern of six beats per line simply does not work as well in English poetry as it does in Greek, Latin, or even French.

There are a lot of repetitive phrases in the *Iliad* and the *Odyssey*. Each time the story's action begins in the morning, Homer always told of the goddess of the Dawn stretching out her rosy fingers or her saffron robes across the sky. Even more notably, each major character's name is complemented with a stock epithet, a repeated formulaic phrase, such as "fair-cheeked Briseis" or "Achilles of the swift feet" or "the crafty Odysseus." The name and epithet would make up half a line, making the oral poet's composition and memorization process much easier. The repetition also helped the audience keep track of the details of the story.

Some characters had a choice of alternate stock epithets to suit a longer or shorter portion of the line needed.

## Themes

The death of Patroclus is seen by Albert Lord as similar to and influenced by the death of Enkidu in the *Epic of Gilgamesh*. Death in battle was horrifying to endure and to witness, as it still is now. But a warrior of ancient Greece or Troy was taught to be willing to risk injury and death not only to defend his home city-state but to possibly earn glory and praise. Achilles had been given a prophecy that he could have either a long and prosperous life with no glory, or an early death in battle, though he would always be remembered—but he had believed his friend Patroclus had no such doom and could return home after the war ended.

In an epic that describes hundreds of deaths by bronze swords, spears, and arrows, often including grisly details or such stock epithets as "gashed with the mangling bronze," Briseis' lament is striking. It is about a personal loss, not glory won. Like the Trojan women Andromache and Queen Hecuba, she is most affected by the loss of a kind and trustworthy protector and does not praise him for fighting.

## Commentary

Though shocking behavior to modern readers, it was considered appropriate by ancient Greeks for a woman to tear her skin with her nails in a display of grief at the death of a family member or a spouse. This brief sequence in the long epic intrigued many poets and writers, most recently novelist Dave Duncan, who wondered why the lovely Briseis, unscarred after the deaths of her husband and brothers, would tear her cheeks for Patroclus, who was not her lover Achilles. Using the pen name Sarah B. Franklin, he wrote a novel telling the story of the Trojan War from the point of view of Briseis. This retelling follows in the literary footsteps of medieval poets and Shakespeare's own *Troilus and Cressida*, which usually combine the characters of Chryseis and Briseis.

*Excerpt from the Odyssey, Book 9, lines 577–623*

# Odysseus and his crew escape from the Cyclops

(translated by Ian Johnston)

*… As soon as rose-fingered early Dawn appeared,*
*males in the flock trotted off to pasture,*
*while the females, who had not been milked*
*and thus whose udders were about to burst,*
*bleated in their pens. Their master, in great pain,*
*ran his hands across the backs of all his sheep*
*as they moved past him, but was such a fool,*
*he didn't notice how my men were tied*
*underneath their bellies. Of that flock*
*my ram was the last to move out through the door,*
*weighed down by its thick fleece and my sly thoughts.*
*Mighty Polyphemus, as he stroked its back,*
*spoke to the animal:*

> *"My lovely ram,*
> *why are you the last one in the flock*
> *to come out of the cave? Not once before*
> *have you ever lagged behind the sheep.*
> *No. You've always been well out in front,*
> *striding off to graze on tender shoots of grass*
> *and be the first to reach the river's stream.*
> *You're the one who longs to get back home,*
> *once evening comes, before the others.*
> *But now you're last of all. You must be sad,*
> *grieving for your master's eye, now blinded*
> *by that evil fellow with his hateful crew.*
> *That Nobody destroyed my wits with wine.*
> *But, I tell you, he's not yet escaped being killed.*
> *If only you could feel and speak like me—*
> *you'd tell me where he's hiding from my rage.*
> *I'd smash his brains out on the ground in here,*
> *sprinkle them in every corner of this cave,*
> *and then my heart would ease the agonies*
> *this worthless Nobody has brought on me."*

## Critical Response To Homer

The academic study of Homeric epic poetry, called Homeric scholarship, is part of classical studies. Dating back to antiquity, this discipline is one of the very oldest topics in all scholarship and science. It is one of the largest of all literary disciplines, and the volume of annual publications in print and on the Internet rivals that on Shakespeare. Public libraries even in small cities may have as many as twenty different translations of the *Iliad* and the *Odyssey* in prose or poetry.

There are some truthfully historic elements in Homer's poetry, proven by much research before and after the archaeologist Schliemann found the ruins of Troy. But these epic poems are more useful for helping modern readers understand the cultural goals of the ancient Greeks than their actual history. "The Greek gods and goddesses also take active parts in the stories, and it is in the *Iliad* and the *Odyssey* that we meet with the Olympians … among other divinities, and the very character and attributes of the gods and goddesses are codified," says the Mythography Web site. "The *Iliad* and the *Odyssey* are perhaps our best sources for information on a significant number of mythological figures."[2]

## Suggested Further Reading

Well worth reading are the modern versions of the Homeric stories, such as the novel *Daughter of Troy* by Sarah B. Franklin, *The Firebrand* by Marion Zimmer Bradley, Christopher Logue's retelling of the *Iliad* in *All Day Permanent Red* and *War Music*, and Dan Simmon's science fiction novel *Illium.* Homer's contemporary, Hesiod, also wrote poetry defining the natures of the Greek gods and goddesses.

# 4

# DU FU

## (712–770 C.E.)

Du Fu (also translated as Tu Fu) was born in 712 C.E. in the Gong prefecture, near the capital of Chang'an in what is now Gong County, Henan, China. His mother died shortly after he was born, and his aunt helped to raise him. His grandfather, Du Shenyan, was an official for Empress Wu and a famous poet.

Little is recorded of Du Fu's youth, except that he began writing poetry at the age of seven, and he read thousands of books. He went to the capital in 735 but failed the examination for a government post. Traveling to the northeast to visit his father serving in a provincial post, Du Fu spent much of the next few years enjoying the sports of horseback riding, hunting, falconry, and archery.

The death of his father in 740 made Du Fu the head of his family. He had to

Du Fu

provide for them, but official employment as a government official was impossible. In 743, he earned a meager income as a secretary drafting documents for officials in Luoyang. During the summer of 744, Du Fu attended the funeral of his step-grandmother in Chenliu near Luoyang, and there he met the poet Li Po for the first time. Du Fu had no reputation yet as a poet, and Li Po was already a celebrity, but they became friends, even though they were able to meet only once more during their lives.

Journeying to the capital in 745, Du Fu saw that many of his friends had been banished, executed, or even driven to suicide by the actions of a political clique led by Li Linfu, the prime minister. This troubled him deeply. He wanted to be an official helping the government and the emperor manage the country well.

Du Fu took the exam a second time in 747. Although the prime minister failed all the candidates, Emperor Xuanzong was impressed by samples of Du Fu's writing. At his orders, Du Fu took another

## FACTS

### Du Fu and Free Speech

As well as learning to speak his mind about the injustices he was seeing, Du Fu had to learn to avoid offending any political faction. By trying too hard to be in the right place saying the right thing, he once got himself arrested for speaking out in a friend's defense on a civil case, and on another occasion he was captured by raiders and held prisoner. He learned the merits of veiling his advice in enigmatic poetry when circumstances warranted, though he could still be frank with acquaintances.

examination and was allowed to wait for a position to become vacant. Three years later, he was appointed to a modest position, after his family suffered bitterly from poverty waiting for bureaucratic action. His disappointment enabled him to see that the upper classes often lived in comfort while the poor and the ordinary people suffered nearby. Du Fu married around 752; he and his wife had three sons and two daughters by 757.

Under the looming rebellion of An Lushan, a Turkish general in service to the emperor, Du Fu moved his wife and children to a town out of the capital. "His young son died of starvation before he arrived in Fengxian," reported one commentator. But rather than write of his grief, Du Fu "expresse[d] indignation at the plight of ordinary people who, unlike him, were unable to be excused from taxes or military service.… Du Fu is the only poet of his time who wrote directly about the events of the An Lushan Rebellion. [As well,] Du Fu is the first poet of the Chinese literary tradition to write extensively about his wife and children."[1]

Disillusioned with official service, he resigned his post and took his family as refugees to Qinzhou. In this frontier city, he had relatives and friends. He did some work there as a consultant for the ministry of public works but largely survived on the financial support of the military governor Yan Wu, who was his friend. After Yan Wu died, Du Fu moved his family to Kuizhou on the gorges of the Yangtze River. Another friend became the governor there and was able to employ Du Fu as a secretary. During the two years he lived there, he wrote more than four hundred poems, nearly a third of his surviving poems, over fourteen hundred in all.

In 768, Du Fu set off down the Yangtze with his wife and sons. He traveled during the next two years, hampered by ill health and unable to reach the capital because of incursions by Tibetan raiders. He died in November or December 770, near Tanzhou (modern Changsha).

# Day's End

(translated by David Hinton)

*Oxen and sheep were brought back down*
*Long ago, and bramble gates closed. Over*
*Mountains and rivers, far from my old garden,*
*A windswept moon rises into clear night.*

*Springs trickle down dark cliffs, and autumn*
*Dew fills ridgeline grasses. My hair seems*
*Whiter in lamplight. The flame flickers*
*Good fortune over and over—and for what?*

## Summary and Explication

The narrator describes the view, looking out from his garden over mountains and rivers at the moon, and back down the cliffs to dewy grasses. The lamp is decorated with the character for good fortune (either painted on a translucent diffuser or cut out of a porcelain shell) to encourage a positive attitude, but it does not give him hope.

## Poetic Techniques

In his later years, the poet took to writing quatrains and octaves like this verse of eight short, formal lines instead of long and detailed ballads. This octave is a lushi, a poetic form that has five characters to the line and parallels between the lines in the second and third couplets, which had to have contrasting subject matter. (Many of the requirements for this poetic form have been lost in the translation to English.)

   "In the literary matters of innovative technique and the establishment of many new subgenres, Du Fu is … seen as without peer: his precedent was influential equally in setting a poetic rule and in breaking it," wrote one critic. "In the allusive, imitation-based tradition of classical poetry, his work constituted an endless source of quotation and precedent, the lines studied and imitated, the imagery echoed, the subgenres enlarged."[2]

## Themes

Chinese poetry is written with a different mindset from its Western counterpart and was already thousands of years old when Indo-European barbarians like Homer were learning to use stock epithets in oral composition. Each written character is not a symbol for a sound; instead, it represents a word and evokes a picture for the reader. The characters have remained essentially unchanged for thousands of years, and so each has become associated with an emotional charge and has accumulated multiple associated significances from earlier works of poetry and prose. Just as the word "solidarity" has accumulated associated meanings in the West since the rise of the unions and since the political movement in Poland in the latter part of the twentieth century, so each of the words the poet has chosen for this brief poem is intended to evoke in his reader echoes of significant verse by earlier poets.

A Western reader unfamiliar with the history of poetry paradigms used by Du Fu would have to concentrate on the pastoral imagery and the suggestions that the narrator is aging. The symbol of Good Fortune on the narrator's lamp flickers as the flame flutters in the evening breeze. Is good fortune at hand or fading away? Is this a poem of evening peace and acceptance, or is it one of despair as time lays its hand on the narrator? It is most certainly an ambivalent poem.

## Commentary

A student of English literature, even at the beginning of her or his studies, can probably recognize a few quotes from Shakespeare or the Bible. But the same student reading this poem by Du Fu would be much more likely to be unconscious of all the references to classic Chinese poetry. The poem would have to be read in isolation, not as part of a commentary on a culture, and it would have to stand on its own merits.

And it does. In this brief poem, by speaking of the shutting of the primitive-style gate to keep in domesticated animals and to keep out wild beasts, by using water imagery and the rising moon over mountains and then focusing on small grasses and his own white hair, the poet takes the reader from his garden to look out across the wide wilderness and back to his own garden and the lamp flickering at his hand. The reader can imagine what the poet sees. What is being described here is not only the poet's eyes moving from garden to the moon and back. It is a journey of the mind, covering not only the time span from the beginning of human history (with the domestication of animals inside bramble fences) to civilized China, but also the timeless shaping of mountains and rivers and the turning of the season. Small wonder if the narrator feels his age and wonders what he has done to make or earn good fortune.

# Alone, Looking for Blossoms Along the River

(translated by David Hinton)

The sorrow of riverside blossoms inexplicable,
And nowhere to complain—I've gone half crazy.
I look up our southern neighbor. But my friend in wine
Gone ten days drinking. I find only an empty bed.

A thick frenzy of blossoms shrouding the riverside,
I stroll, listing dangerously, in full fear of spring.
Poems, wine—even this profusely driven, I endure.
Arrangements for this old, white-haired man can wait.

A deep river, two or three houses in bamboo quiet,
And such goings on: red blossoms glaring with white!
Among spring's vociferous glories, I too have my place:
With a lovely wine, bidding life's affairs bon voyage.

Looking east to Shao, its smoke filled with blossoms,
I admire that stately Po-hua wineshop even more.
To empty golden wine cups, calling such beautiful
Dancing girls to embroidered mats—who could bear it?

East of the river, before Abbot Huang's grave,
Spring is a frail splendor among gentle breezes.
In this crush of peach blossoms opening ownerless,
Shall I treasure light reds, or treasure them dark?

At Madame Huang's house, blossoms fill the paths:
Thousands, tens of thousands haul the branches down.
And butterflies linger playfully—an unbroken
Dance floating to songs orioles sing at their ease.

I don't so love blossoms I want to die. I'm afraid,
Once they are gone, of old age still more impetuous.
And they scatter gladly, by the branchful. Let's talk
Things over, little buds—open delicately, sparingly.

# By the Lake

(translated by David Hawkes)

*The old fellow from Shao-ling weeps with stifled sobs as he walks furtively by the bends of the Sepentine on a day in spring. In the waterside palaces the thousands of doors are locked. For whom have the willows and rushes put on their fresh greenery?*

*I remember how formerly, when the Emperor's rainbow banner made its way into the South Park, everything in the park seemed to bloom with a brighter color. The First Lady of the Chao-yang Palace rode in the same carriage as her lord in attendance at his side, while before the carriage rode maids of honor equipped with bows and arrows, their white horses champing at golden bits. Leaning back, face skywards, they shot into the clouds; and the Lady laughed gaily when a bird fell to the ground transfixed by a well-aimed arrow. Where are the bright eyes and the flashing smile now? Tainted with blood-pollution, her wandering soul cannot make its way back.*

*The clear waters of the Wei flow eastwards, and Chien-ko is far away: between the one who has gone and the one who remains no communication is possible. It is human to have feelings and shed tears for such things; but the grasses and flowers of the lakeside go on for ever, unmoved. As evening falls, the city is full of the dust of foreign horseman. My way is towards the South City, but my gaze turns northward.*

**blood-pollution**—guilt and shame from having killed a person or
        animal, in this case the bird

## CriTicaL Response To Du Fu

Though he was thought of with affection by his contemporaries, Du Fu was not considered an important poet during his lifetime. However, he had great and lasting influence on Chinese poetry. Later poets in the T'ang dynasty wrote protest poems inspired by his style. He rose to lasting prominence when the history of poetry during the T'ang dynasty was written during the later Sung dynasty, becoming known as the poet historian or even the sage of poetry. According to biographer Eva Shan Chou:

> Admiration for Tu Fu's technical brilliance and for the moral excellence of his character combined to raise him from relative obscurity to the apex of T'ang poetry. His work, and that of his contemporary Li Po, defined the boundaries of the High T'ang period, and this period in turn came to be identified with the extraordinary flourishing of culture and political power seen in the middle decades of the eighth century.... In Tu Fu's work, [the literary establishment] found a poet who was able to satisfy all the levels—aesthetic, moral, and human—on which the traditional scholar-official defined himself.[3]

In China, by the fourteenth century, critical works on the poetry of Du Fu far outnumbered works on any other poet. With each passing century, the number of scholarly works on this honored poet increases and multiplies to an extent that exceeds that written in the West on Homer or Shakespeare. Recognized as perhaps the greatest poet of the Chinese tradition, Du Fu's works have been almost canonized, because in them the Chinese mind and moral being are seen as being expressed in their highest form. His poems have a moral supremacy beyond merely literary considerations, and the poet himself is considered to embody unceasing loyalty and public-minded dedication to serve his emperor and his state.

## SuggesTed FurTher Reading

There are many poets held in high esteem in China, among them Li Po, Cui Hao, and Wang Wei. Well worth researching is Iasyr Shivaza, the Chinese-Russian inventor of the Dungan language alphabet.

# 5

# OMAR KHAYYAM

## (1048–1131)

In or around 1048 C.E., Omar Khayyam was born at Nishapur in Khorassan, part of Persia (now Iran). Some authorities consider his date of birth to be 1021. His full name in Arabic was Ghiyath al-Din Abu'l-Fath umar ibn Ibrahim Al-Nisaburi al-Khayyami. His surname al-Khayyami means tent maker, which may have been his father's trade.

The details of Omar's youth have not been recorded, but he appears to have had an excellent education, studying for nine years in Samarkand and Bukhara. He was fluent in both Arabic and Perso-Tajik (a Persian language). One of his teachers in Nishapur was the Iman Mowaffak, and another in Samarkand was Ibn-i Sina. While studying in Samara, Omar completed a treatise on algebra.

In 1074, he was commissioned to build an astronomical observatory in the city of Isfahan in collaboration with other astronomers and to do research. As the astronomer to Sultan Malik Shah, he was one of eight scholars responsible for reforming the old Persian solar calendar, a task comparable to the revision of the Julian calendar by Pope Gregory. The result of their five years of work was the adoption on March 15, 1079, of a new calendar reckoning, the so-called Jalalian or Seljuk era. This calendar version was later discontinued for a time but restored in Iran in 1925. Omar also completed organizing the results of the group's astronomical research. Granted a pension by the Vizier Nizam al-Mulk, for nearly twenty years Omar was able to devote himself to learning and research, writing books on philosophy, physics, mathematics, geography, astronomy, history, and music.

A painting showing Omar Khayyam. He was an accomplished mathematician and scientist as well as a poet.

Omar wrote many important mathematical studies advancing the knowledge of algebra, creating and resolving a number of equations, which European mathematicians were unable to resolve until four and five hundred years later. His study *The Difficulties of Euclid's Definitions* and his textbook on algebra were advanced beyond European studies of mathematics. He was celebrated beyond Bukhara and Khurasan as the greatest mathematician of his time.

Belonging to the philosophic school of Avicenna, Omar taught Greek science. He had an excellent memory and unrivaled knowledge of astronomy and philosophy, but he is reported to have been an ill-tempered miser who disliked teaching. His home was frequently a salon for discussion of scientific and philosophical matters as well as poetry. Among the authorities who were Omar's contemporaries or lived within 150 years of his death, the consensus is that "Omar was pre-eminently a man of science … one who drank deep at the well of Greek wisdom, and composed many famous works on astronomy, mathematics, metaphysics and natural philosophy."[1]

Politics made the life of an educated man difficult at that time. Among Omar's responsibilities at the court of Sultan Malik Shah were those of an astrologer. He was once called upon to predict an auspicious day for a festival. The date Omar selected did indeed enjoy fair weather, and he was praised by all attending; but even the sultan knew that the selection owed less to the casting of a horoscope than it did to Omar's studies in astronomy and weather prediction. It was not politic or appropriate, though, for Omar to admit publicly that he did not believe in astrology, as he already offended too many conservatives with his other opinions.

Omar was born to a family that practiced Sufism, a mystical form of Islam, but his writings showed that his religious beliefs were not particularly orthodox. Protected by the court, Omar expressed his philosophical opinions openly in five books that showed original thought as well as following the teachings of the masha' philosophers, Islamic scholars of Plato. His works were discussed widely by other students of the same masters. Like Avicenna, an earlier scholar of that time, Omar was condemned by the influential philosopher Abu Hamid al-Ghazali as being in conflict with the fundamentals of religion. His verses were considered errors in the eyes of the canon law.

In 1092, after the deaths of Omar's patron, Nizam al-Mulk, and Sultan Malik Shah, the Isfahan observatory was closed by the new sultan Sanjar, who summoned Omar to the new capital in Merv. After staying there for a while, he returned to Nishapur, but the city erupted with religious strife in 1095, and those with masha'i ideas were persecuted. Omar took this opportunity to make the pilgrimage to Mecca as is expected of every devout Muslim, but during his return to Nishapur after the unrest ended, he offended some of his associates by not making as many social visits as was expected of a scholar and a gentleman.

Omar is recorded as having told one of his pupils, during a conversation in a garden, that he had chosen the site for his grave in Nisapur, in a spot where the north wind would scatter roses over his tomb. He died at home in 1131 (some authorities report it as early as 1122), after reading Avicenna's *Book of Healing* and calling his household to hear his will and last prayer.

# FACTS

## FitzGerald and the *Rubaiyat*

In March 1857, Professor Edward Byles Cowell of Cambridge visited the Asiatic Society library in Calcutta, where he discovered Omar's *Rubaiyat*. He sent a copy to his former student, Edward FitzGerald, in England. FitzGerald published a freely paraphrased English translation of the *Rubaiyat* of Omar Khayyam in January 1859. The most complete collection preserved has eight hundred independent quatrain verses, arranged in order of their rhymes. FitzGerald chose seventy-five verses and arranged them in an order that made thematic sense to him.

Many of the verses have missing or misspelled words in the original Farsi. Three-quarters or more have been shown to be written by other writers and added at a later date. The oldest manuscript preserved has 158 verses, but it is dated 1461 c.e., some three and a half centuries after Omar's death, and at least 16 verses are by other authors. At this point, it is impossible to confirm more than one or two of the verses as the work of Omar the astronomer and philosopher. In Western countries, FitzGerald's paraphrased translation of the *Rubaiyat* is far more famous than any of Omar's scientific works.

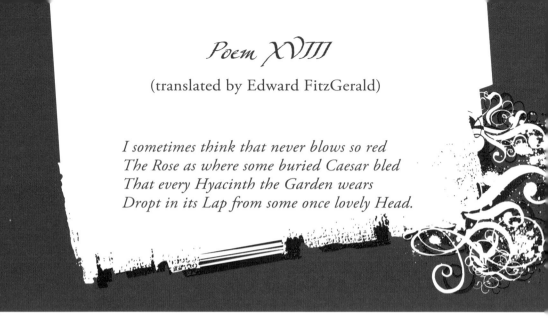

# Poem XVIII

## (translated by Edward FitzGerald)

*I sometimes think that never blows so red*
*The Rose as where some buried Caesar bled*
*That every Hyacinth the Garden wears*
*Dropt in its Lap from some once lovely Head.*

## Summary and Explication

A plain translation of the original verse, more literal than this poem, has been done by Cambridge lecturer Reynold Alleyne Nicholson:

"Wherever roses and tulips bloom

They spring from the red blood of a mighty king.

Every violet that grows from the earth

Was once a mole on the cheek of a beauty."[2]

## Poetic Techniques

Omar wrote in four-line verses called *ruba'i*, an Arabic word for "foursome." In these *rubaiyat*, the first, second, and fourth lines of these epigrammatic quatrain verses must rhyme. A ruba'i is usually composed of two phrases that complete a verse.

In this verse, the poet and translator each chose particular words for "king" and for "flowers," words that evoke legendary figures from myth and history.

## Themes

Omar's verses are often about superficially trivial things, such as flowers or clay pots. But as the *Columbia Encyclopedia* listing points out: "The hedonism of his verse often masks his serious reflections on metaphysical issues."[3] The primary themes in this brief verse are universal mortality, which takes even great kings and evanescent beauties. But the natural world renews new life out of death. It used to be believed that true kings could heal by the laying on of hands; and at any rate, the deeds of monarchs, whether good or bad, battles or healing, all come to dust. Mighty deeds, whether good or evil, are no more lasting than human beauty or fair flowers, which are all recycled by the restorative composting of the natural world.

## Commentary

This verse is worth comparing to Genesis 3:19 from the King James Bible: "In the sweat of thy face shalt thou eat bread, till thou return unto the ground; for out of it wast thou taken: for dust thou art, and unto dust shalt thou return."[4] As an educated Muslim, Omar would have been familiar with Genesis and the other books of the Hebrew Torah, which later became part of the Old Testament of the Bible.

Omar's verses are interpreted as synthesizing the thoughts of Plato, Aristotle, al-Farabi, and Omar's master Ibn-i Sina, reiterating masha'i beliefs discussing cause and effect and the necessity of Creation.

*Poem XI*
(translated by Edward FitzGerald)

*Here with a Loaf of Bread beneath the Bough,*
*A Flask of Wine, a Book of Verse—and Thou*
*Beside me singing in the Wilderness—*
*And Wilderness is Paradise enow.*

**enow**—enough

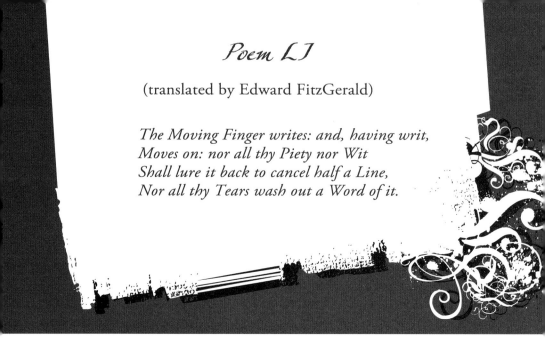

# Poem LI

## (translated by Edward FitzGerald)

*The Moving Finger writes: and, having writ,*
*Moves on: nor all thy Piety nor Wit*
*Shall lure it back to cancel half a Line,*
*Nor all thy Tears wash out a Word of it.*

## Critical Response To Omar

Biographies of Omar usually report that European readers and critics had not heard of the *Rubaiyat* until FitzGerald's paraphrased translation in 1859. But a dedicated reading of the poetry of Edmund Spenser (1552–1599) and the ending of *Candide* by Voltaire (1694–1778) shows themes and phrases evocative of the *Rubaiyat*. It is entirely possible the *Rubaiyat* was available to a few educated Europeans, perhaps brought to the West by alchemists and mathematicians.

Nicholson reports that among his contemporaries and biographers, Omar was "reckoned among those unfortunate 'philosophers and materialists' who have gone astray from the Truth."[5] Modern scholars and poets are less concerned with orthodoxy and more with the perceptive analyses of human behavior in these epigrammatic verses, which range from bawdy to subtle and have wide appeal to readers. As one commentator noted, "The Rubaiyat of Omar Khayyam is among the few masterpieces that has been translated into most languages, including English, French, German, Italian, Russian, Chinese, Hindi, Arabic and Urdu."[6]

## Suggested Further Reading

Readers who enjoy Omar's *Rubaiyat* could try the poetry of Ovid and Sophocles and Horace, and also of Kahlil Gibran.

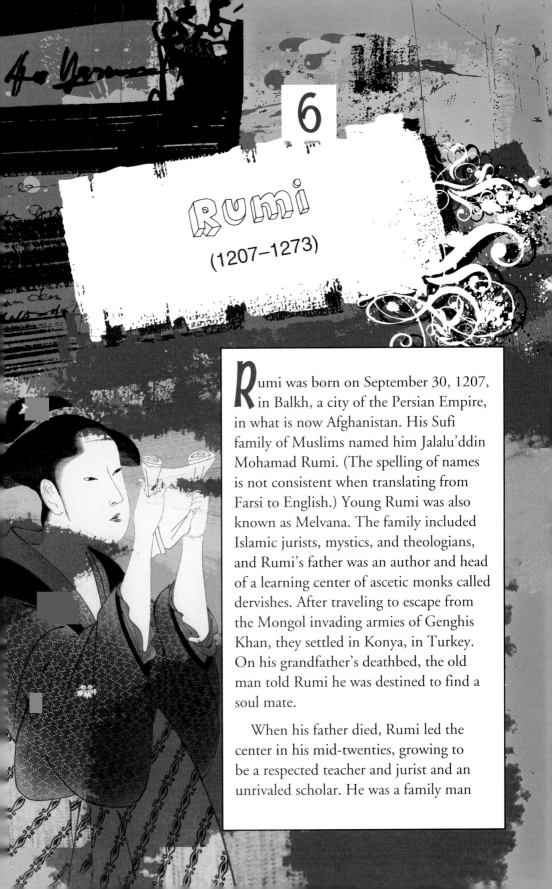

# 6

# Rumi
## (1207–1273)

**R**umi was born on September 30, 1207, in Balkh, a city of the Persian Empire, in what is now Afghanistan. His Sufi family of Muslims named him Jalalu'ddin Mohamad Rumi. (The spelling of names is not consistent when translating from Farsi to English.) Young Rumi was also known as Melvana. The family included Islamic jurists, mystics, and theologians, and Rumi's father was an author and head of a learning center of ascetic monks called dervishes. After traveling to escape from the Mongol invading armies of Genghis Khan, they settled in Konya, in Turkey. On his grandfather's deathbed, the old man told Rumi he was destined to find a soul mate.

When his father died, Rumi led the center in his mid-twenties, growing to be a respected teacher and jurist and an unrivaled scholar. He was a family man

Jalalu'ddin Mohamad Rumi

who raised four children and married a second time after the death of his first wife. "Then one day he met a wandering dervish, a man who was very sensitive to the cold, and older than Rumi was," says Jean Claude Carriere in his introduction to *Love: The Joy That Wounds*. "He spoke in riddles, was insolent and irritable, and his name was Shams al-din of Tabris. Love blossomed between the two men. They stayed together, locked away, for forty days and forty nights."[1]

The students in Rumi's large household did not like that this rough, uncompromising stranger had such influence over their leader, and they pressured him to leave. But Rumi followed him and got him to return to his home, where Shams married a young woman of the household. When Shams was pressured again into leaving, Rumi searched for him again as far as Damascus before abandoning the search. If his students had made Shams disappear, it was a failure, for Rumi had realized that he possessed his beloved in his heart.

He was now a poet, a whirling dancer, and a painter in ecstatic union with God through his beloved friend. With one hand on a post, he would walk in circles and recite verse after verse, inspired by love and reverence.

Rumi became a grand master of the Sufi mystic tradition and founder of the brotherhood of Whirling Dervishes. He died on December 17, 1273, and a tomb was built for him in Konya, Turkey, beside the grave of his father.

# FACTS

## Rumi and Religion

Rumi was renowned for his acceptance of all religions and beliefs and is quoted as saying "Christian, Jew, Muslim, shaman, Zoroastrian, stone, ground, mountain, river, each has a secret way of being with the mystery, unique and not to be judged."[2] At his funeral, he was honored by Muslims, Christians, Jews, Arabs, Persians, Turks, and Romans.

Excerpt from

# A Sleep and a Forgetting

(translated by Tajadad and Powell)

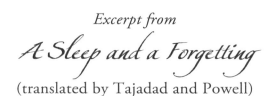

*One who has lived many years in a city,*
*as soon as he goes to sleep,*
  *Beholds another city full of good and evil,*
*and his own city vanishes from his mind.*
  *He does not say to himself,*
*"This is a new city. I am a stranger here,"*
  *He thinks he has always lived in this city*
*and was born and bred in it.*
  *What wonder, then, if the soul does not remember*
*her ancient abode and birthplace?*
  *Since she is wrapped in the slumber of this world,*
*like a star covered by clouds?—*
  *Especially as she has trodden so many cities*
*and the dust that darkens her vision*
*is not yet swept away.*

## Summary and Explication

The poet describes how a person can dream of a city and in the dream, forgets his own city. It's no wonder, then, that people do not remember what happened before they were born, especially since they have lived so many lives in the past and are confused by living in this body right now.

## Poetic Techniques

This verse begins in a storytelling fashion, making statements as if telling the story of someone who had this dream. The words are short, plain, and direct. The tone shifts abruptly then as the poet asks, "What wonder, then …" as more of the words become longer, more evocative, and less simple. The poet is asking rhetorical questions here, and the phrasing is more complex than in the first lines. It is interesting that instead of making flat statements that the soul does not remember where she once lived because she is asleep now, the poet phrases these lines as questions. This technique suggests both that the poet is framing his material in the format of teaching questions, like Socrates, and that the poet is inviting the reader to agree.

## Themes

The dominant theme here is the mystic idea that not only are people preexisting souls that have been born into their bodies, forgetting their past, but that being born is like falling asleep—it is not one's active existence, in which one faces reality and has real accomplishments. This belief separating sleep and dreams from one's real life is not a universal perspective among all cultures; it is a Platonic idea. Plato's teaching story (of humanity living in a cave and seeing shadows on the cave wall instead of real objects) spread with Greek philosophy. It differs from earlier beliefs in the Middle East as well as elsewhere in the world.

The title was added later by a translator and is from the first line of William Wordsworth's poem "Ode on Intimations of Immortality." This addition was a perceptive interpretation of this poem's imagery.

## Commentary

From this verse, it is clear that Rumi's studies included Greek philosophy and the works of Plato. It is fascinating to see such a clear example of how teaching materials are reinterpreted by people in different cultures from their own perspectives. This poem shows that Rumi thought of the world as a dreamlike distraction from the real origins and goals of the human soul.

But Rumi was not only a dry student of books, who interpreted the law coldly without embracing the things of this world. Maryam Mafi and Azima Melita Kolin say in their book *Rumi: Hidden Music* that Shams showed Rumi "an ecstatic way of worship through poetry, music, Sama or meditative whirling and freed him from the restraints of piety and self-renunciation."[3] He did not have to renounce the world as an unworthy distraction; he could seek emotion and ecstasy, the love of his family and friends, and the pleasures of the senses, such as music and dancing.

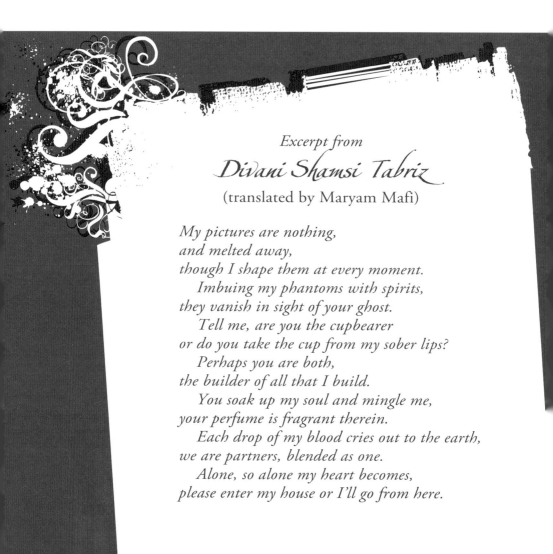

*Excerpt from*

*Divani Shamsi Tabriz*

(translated by Maryam Mafi)

*My pictures are nothing,*
*and melted away,*
*though I shape them at every moment.*
*    Imbuing my phantoms with spirits,*
*they vanish in sight of your ghost.*
*    Tell me, are you the cupbearer*
*or do you take the cup from my sober lips?*
*    Perhaps you are both,*
*the builder of all that I build.*
*    You soak up my soul and mingle me,*
*your perfume is fragrant therein.*
*    Each drop of my blood cries out to the earth,*
*we are partners, blended as one.*
*    Alone, so alone my heart becomes,*
*please enter my house or I'll go from here.*

Excerpt from

# And Patience Flees My Heart

(translated by Tajadad and Powell)

*Desire for your face*
*Would split the hardest stone.*
*Life takes wing and soars,*
*In my joy of having you.*

*Fire becomes like water,*
*My reason is destroyed.*
*And imagining you*
*Kills any hope of sleep.*

## Critical Response To Rumi

Each culture has its own artistic heroes, but the measure of true genius is when the art created transcends language and cultural barriers to succeed outside the place and time where it was made. Jean Claude Carriere considers Rumi's *Masnari* and *The Book of Shams al-Din of Tabriz* to be "two jewels in the world's history of poetry."[4]

Rumi composed some fifty thousand lines of verse and has become the world's best-selling poet. His poems continue to be chanted during religious ceremonies and on pilgrimages.

"Rumi published many great poems, using common everyday objects and circumstances to describe the spiritual world," says one of the online biographies of this popular spiritual leader. "His poems would, and still do reach those that read them on different levels, with common folk relating to the beauty of his words, while those that work harder with their spiritual practices can read of deeper meanings."[5]

## Suggested Further Reading

Other poets who have dedicated their lives to religious studies are interesting, such as the devotional works of Hildegard of Bingen, Mechtild of Magdeburg, or Kahlil Gibran. Also worth reading are Horace as well as Ovid's *Metamorphoses.*

# DANTE

## (1265–1321)

Sometime between May 14 and June 13, 1265, Dante was born in Florence in what is now Italy. He was baptized Durante Alighieri, and Dante seems to have been a nickname. His family were nobles loyal to the Guelphs, a political alliance supporting the Papacy, and they claimed to be descended from the ancient Romans. His father was Alighiero de Bellincione. His mother, Bella degli Abati, died when Dante was seven years old. His father soon married again.

It was love at first sight, without a word spoken, when young Dante met Beatrice Portinari at age nine. But at age twelve, young Dante was promised in marriage to Gemma di Manetto Donati. After he was eighteen, he saw Beatrice again, often exchanging greetings, but kept his distance. Beatrice was his inspiration for several sonnets, but he made no mention of Gemma in his poetry, though they had several children together after their marriage in 1285.

Studying at home, Dante learned of Tuscan and Sicilian poetry, and classic Latin poetry as well as the works of troubadours in Occitan, a language derived from Latin, spoken in what is now southern France. At eighteen, he met Brunetto Latini, Guido Cavalcanti, Lapo Gianni, and Cino da Pistoia. They became a group of poets leading the *Dolce Stil Novo* (The Sweet New Style), and Dante made the passion of his friendly and courtly love for Beatrice his reason for composing poetry. He accepted Beatrice's marriage to Simone dei Bardi in 1287, but when Beatrice died in 1290, he withdrew into classical Latin studies of philosophy and theology.

At the victorious battle of Campaldino, June 11, 1289, Dante fought in the front rank of the Guelph cavalry. As an active council member in the reformed Florentine republic, Dante had to belong to a guild, so he became a pharmacist in the guild of physicians and apothecaries. In 1301, he was part of a delegation sent to Rome to determine the pope's intentions for a visiting papal ambassador to Florence. Pope Boniface insisted that Dante remain. When a new government took over in Florence through a coup, it condemned Dante to

Dante

exile and ordered him to pay a large fine, though all his assets had been seized, and sentenced him to death if he returned.

Dante took part in several unsuccessful attempts by his party to regain power. In 1315, an amnesty was offered to exiles, but Dante refused to pay fines and do public penance. His death sentence was confirmed and extended to his sons. Bitter from the treachery and ineffectiveness of his allies, Dante left all politics.

He began work on his *Divina Commedia* (Divine Comedy) and was encouraged by the response to each of three parts as he wrote it: *Inferno*, *Purgatorio*, and *Paradiso*. In this epic work, the inspirational figure of Beatrice appears as a guide and the final symbol of salvation.

He was able to find patrons among the courts of the northern Italian princes, in Verona, then Sarzana and Lucca. Some sources suggest he visited Paris and Oxford. He moved to Ravenna in 1318 at the invitation of Prince Guido Novello da Polenta. After a diplomatic mission to Venice, Dante died at the age of fifty-six in 1321, possibly of malaria.

# FACTS

## Dante's Tomb

After Dante's death, the city of Florence made repeated official requests to have his remains laid to rest there. In 1519, Pope Leo X decided that Dante's remains should be delivered to Florence so Michelangelo could construct a grand tomb. Custodians of his tomb in the monastery at Ravenna refused, and they even concealed his bones in a false wall. So in 1829, an empty tomb was built in Florence at the basilica of Santa Croce, with an inscription reading "Honor the most exalted poet"—a quote from Dante's *Inferno*, in which the poet Virgil is the most honored of the ancient poets residing in Limbo.

# Inferno, canto 7, verses 25—42

(translated by Henry Wadsworth Longfellow)

Here, more than elsewhere, I saw multitudes
to every side of me; their howls were loud
while, wheeling weights, they used their chests to push.

They struck against each other; at that point,
each turned around and, wheeling back those weights,
cried out: "Why do you hoard?" "Why do you squander?"

So did they move around the sorry circle
from left and right to the opposing point;
again, again they cried their chant of scorn;

and so, when each of them had changed positions,
he circled halfway back to his next joust.
And I, who felt my heart almost pierced through,

requested: "Master, show me now what shades
are these and tell me if they all were cleric—
those tonsured ones who circle on our left."

And he to me: "All these, to left and right
were so squint-eyed of mind in the first life—
no spending that they did was done with measure...."

## Summary and Explication

In this excerpt, the narrator in his vision is being led by Virgil into Hell, where the damned are tormented by the sins they committed in life. Here, in the fourth circle of hell, are the souls of many people pushing with their chests against wheeled carts loaded with heavy weights. They are pushing the carts around in opposing circles until each cart strikes against another, and then each turns around and they push the carts in the opposite directions around the circle until they collide again. The tormented cry out to each other, some saying "Why do you hoard?" and others "Why do you squander?"

The narrator asks who these people are and if all the ones who hoarded were men of the Church. The guide replies that all these people saw the world so wrongly when they were alive, they did not measure out what they spent, to spend the right amount.

## Poetic Techniques

Dante did not choose a simple pattern for the lines of his great work. "Written in a complex pentameter form, terza rima, it is a magnificent synthesis of the medieval outlook, picturing a changeless universe ordered by God," wrote one commentator.[1] The translation gives only some small idea of how these words were carefully chosen for their expressive sounds, as the dialect Dante spoke was far more fluid and mellifluous than modern English. Terza rima was a popular formal pattern of that time for writing long verses and epic poems. Dante made so many changes to this pattern that it is effectively almost a new form of his own devising. This structure focused his thinking, and he was able to write thousands of lines that were well matched for harmonious structure.

## Themes

Greed is the primary theme profiled here. Dante was the first great poet to define both the miser and the prodigal as committing the sin of avarice, or greed and the lust for material gain. The miser spent too little, hoarding money and resources that ought to have been used. The prodigal spent too freely, wasting and squandering money and resources that ought to have been rationed and husbanded. The sin of both the miser and the prodigal was immoderation; they did not measure out with rational judgment an appropriate use and consumption of money and resources.

Dante's condemnation of the sin of avarice in particular runs throughout the *Divine Comedy*, strikingly vicious compared with his attitudes toward lust and gluttony. Consistent with the biblical verse saying that greed for money was the root of all evils (1 Timothy 6:10) and also with medieval Christian commentators who viewed avarice as most offensive to the spirit of love, Dante brought the classical principle of the Golden Mean and moderation to his criticism. In his opinion, the sin was a common vice of monks and church leaders, even cardinals and popes. He thought it fitting that the misers and prodigals should punish and insult each other in the afterlife, and both should be so physically changed by their sins they should be unrecognizable and indistinguishable.

## Commentary

One commentator wrote:

> The "Divina Commedia" is an allegory of human life, in the form of a vision of the world beyond the grave, written avowedly with the object of converting a corrupt society to righteousness.… He is relating, nearly twenty years after the event, a vision which was granted to him (for his own salvation when leading a sinful life) during the year of jubilee, 1300, in which for seven days … he passed through hell, purgatory, and paradise, spoke with the souls in each realm, and heard what the Providence of God had in store for himself and the world.[2]

This is not the story of a man's life or what he thought and believed. It is a narrative meant to show how Dante felt the cosmos ought to work, with justice for wrongs done and rewards for faithfulness.

"The sacred poem, the last book of the Middle Ages, sums up the knowledge and intellectual attainment of the centuries that passed between the fall of the Roman Empire and the beginning of the Renaissance," wrote scholar Russell McNeil, adding, "it gives a complete picture of Catholicism in the thirteenth century in Italy."[3] Dante lived in a time when the Dark Ages were ending. Once again, intellectuals could think and write in ways that considered religious dogma a useful tool, not an end in itself. "The value of Dante lies not in an epic that heavily cribbed notes from the likes of Virgil," according to one recent critic, "rather it lies in his attempt to solidify a definite code of behavior that was to be expected of all men and women of his age."[4]

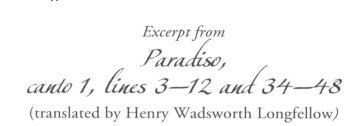

Excerpt from
*Paradiso,*
canto 1, lines 3—12 and 34—48
(translated by Henry Wadsworth Longfellow)

*To course across more kindly waters now*
*my talent's little vessel lifts her sails,*
*leaving behind herself a sea so cruel;*

*and what I sing will be that second kingdom,*
*in which the human soul is cleansed of sin,*
*becoming worthy of ascent to Heaven.*

*But here, since I am yours, O holy Muses,*
*may this poem rise again from Hell's dead realm;*
*and may Calliope rise somewhat here,*

*accompanying my singing with that music*
*whose power struck the poor Pierides*
*so forcefully that they despaired of pardon....*

*... Great fire can follow a small spark: there may*
*be better voices after me to pray*
*to Cyrrha's god for aid—that he may answer.*

*The lantern of the world approaches mortals*
*by varied paths; but on that way which links*
*four circles with three crosses, it emerges*

*joined to a better constellation and*
*along a better course, and it can temper*
*and stamp the world's wax more in its own manner.*

*Its entry from that point of the horizon*
*brought morning there and evening here; almost*
*all of that hemisphere was white—while ours*

*was dark—when I saw Beatrice turn round*
*and left, that she might see the sun; no eagle*

**Calliope**—the Muse of epic poetry

**Pierides**—another name for the Muses

**Cyrrha's god**—the god Apollo is associated with the mountain peak of Parnassus called Cyrrha.

**The lantern of the world … manner**—The sun's apparent path across the sky changes daily, and on the spring equinox the sun appears in the constellation Aries as it was when God created the universe, so the world is more favorably influenced by the sun.

## Critical Response To Dante

The major poets and writers of Western European countries have all been strongly influenced by Dante. Before Dante, educated European poets composed verses in Latin, which they considered the only language proper for formal poetry, not doggerel in the local dialects or barbarian languages. He was one of the first poets to write and publish verse in the dialect of his home city-state and to compose surpassingly well. The modern Italian language has taken its form from the dialect that Dante used: The educated people of the city-states of what eventually became the modern country of Italy so admired Dante's work that they not only read it and talked about it, they changed their own dialects to be more like his.

When the King's English gradually took precedence over the other four dialects of English being used at the time of Shakespeare, certainly the publication of Shakespeare's plays in the dialect spoken in and around London contributed to the change, though not as much as the English translation of the King James Bible. But in Italy, the work of their honored poet Dante and his colleagues was itself the focus for the language change: The people wanted to talk and write like Dante. And as the works of the Italian Renaissance spread outward through Europe from Italy, many educated people coveted a Dante in their own languages, and some poets aspired to be a Dante, rather than a Virgil writing in Latin.

## Suggested Further Reading

In English, the influence of Dante can be traced in the works of Chaucer, Shakespeare, and Milton. Just as the troubadours of the area that later became southern France had an influence on Dante, so his writing had influence on the *chansons de geste* (songs of heroes' quests) in French and later on the works of Verlaine and Rimbaud. In German, his influence can be found in Goethe's writing.

# 8

# BASHŌ

## (1644–1694)

Bashō was the pen name of Matsuo Kinsaku, born in 1644 near Ueno in Japan. His father was Matsuo Yozaemon, a samurai of low rank; in peacetime he was a farmer. Young Matsuo was the second son, and he had four sisters.

The Matsuo family's modest but respectable social rank gained their younger son, before his father's death in 1656, a position as companion in service to Todo Yoshitada, a young relative of the province's feudal lord. Together the young men wrote verses, as was fashionable for sophisticated men in Japan. Under the pen name Sobo, young Matsuo even had a few verses published in 1662, 1664, and 1665. At his coming of age, he took the samurai name Matsuo Munefusa.

But in the summer of 1666, his friend and master, Yoshitada, died suddenly and

A statue of Bashō in Japan

prematurely. When Yoshitada's younger brother became head of the clan and husband to the widow, this may have caused many political changes locally. Shortly afterward, Matsuo left Ueno; traditional biographies say he went to the capital of Japan, Kyoto, and studied philosophy, poetry, and calligraphy.

In Kyoto, Matsuo gradually became known among the poets, and many of his verses appeared in four anthologies between 1667 and 1671. When he compiled a book of poetry in 1672, thirty poets contributed verses that were matched in pairs and judged by him in critical comments revealing his colorful wit and knowledge of fashionable expressions and popular songs. That spring, he journeyed to Edo.

For the next eight years he lived there, and he may have earned his living in the local waterworks department. Using the pen name Tosei, he joined other poets in composing renku, collections of a hundred short verses; his work began to appear more and more frequently in anthologies. He was recognized as a master when he distributed a small book of verses among his acquaintances in 1675. He judged several haiku contests and had twenty or more students.

These talented and admiring students built a small house for him in a rustic area near Edo, in 1680 when he was thirty-six years old. Months later, one of his students planted a banana tree beside the hut. He was delighted with the gift and enjoyed the sounds of rainwater dripping from the broad leaves. Soon, visitors began referring to his residence as the Bashō (banana plant) Hut and to him as Master Bashō. He lived in poverty, but happily, sustained by a modest patronage and by donations from his students. Bashō began practicing Zen meditation with Butcho, a priest living nearby, who may have helped him in dealing with feelings of melancholy or loneliness.

When a fire swept through the neighborhood in 1682, the Bashō Hut was destroyed. The news from Bashō's family home in Ueno was also sad, as he received word his mother had died. Still, he kept writing, collecting another anthology with his students the next summer. When he returned from visiting Kai Province, his friends presented him with a new Bashō Hut. But he had become a wanderer in his heart.

In 1684, he began the first of several long journeys on foot, throughout many provinces of Japan, which were inspirational for his contemplative poetry and his other writing. Traveling in Japan was not safe at that time, and there was a high risk of being robbed or murdered. As well, Bashō suffered several chronic illnesses and had a delicate constitution. During these challenging journeys, alone or accompanied by one friend, he would visit the homes of friends and patrons.

His friends and students built him a third Bashō Hut in Edo in 1691, but he had less peace and solitude there. Bashō had people to look after now: an invalid nephew who lived with Bashō, dying in 1693, and a woman named Jutei, who had had a close relationship with Bashō in his youth. One of her sons, Jirobei, traveled with Bashō in 1694. Bashō's health gradually failed during this last journey, and he died in Osaka on November 28 of a stomach ailment.

# FACTS

## Bashō's Gate

In 1693, Bashō was kept very busy with almost daily interruptions from visitors. If he went out to visit others, he felt he was interfering with their business. Resolving to embrace isolation, that fall he put a bolt on his garden gate. About a month later, he was able to reopen the gate, having restored his mental equilibrium. Through *karumi*, a Buddhist philosophy of greeting the mundane world rather than separating from it, he became less attached to worldly concerns. Writing under this principle, his poems began to show lighthearted humor without sentimentalism.

## First Poem

*The old pond*
*a frog jumps in*
*the sound of water*

(translated by R. H. Blyth)


*Old pond*
*leap—splash*
*a frog.*

(translated by Lucien Stryk)


*Old dark sleepy pool*
*quick unexpected frog*
*goes plop! Watersplash.*

(translated by Peter Beilenson)

## Summary and Explication

The seven words of this poem (*furuike ya / kawazu tobikomu / mizu no oto*)
translate most simply as "old pond / frog jumps in / water's sound." But
for an attentive reader, many feelings are evoked by associated meanings of
the words.

## Poetic Techniques

The *haiku* form is derived from the *haikai no renga*, a poetic form with two separate verses. The hokku verse has three lines of five, seven, and five syllables, and it is followed by a pair of lines, usually composed by another poet in collaboration with the first as a dialogue. Bashō is considered to have perfected the hokku and to have set it apart as a distinct, focused form. Masaoka Shiki is credited with inventing in the late nineteenth century the term *haiku* for the freestanding *hokku* verse as composed by Bashō and others.

There are several rules for making a haiku. Though it must have seventeen syllables, the Japanese definition of "syllable" is not identical to English. As well, there must be a *kigo* word, which evokes the season of the year, and through it nature and the seasons of our lives; and there must be a *kake kotoba* word, which is a pivot point or hinge of the poem, where the focus of the poem shifts meaningfully. This pivot word is frequently one with two or more meanings. Japanese has many more homonyms—words spelled alike but different in meaning, such as quail (a bird) and quail (to falter)—and homophones—words pronounced the same but with different spellings and meanings, such as rows and rose—than English does.

Ideally, a haiku is expected to evoke mood and emotion in a contrasting pair of images: One suggests the place and time, and the other makes a brief, vivid observation. The connection is not overt but is left for the reader to perceive.

## Themes

Bashō chooses two terms here from a poetic vocabulary instead of the everyday plain terms commonly used in ordinary speech. The first, *furuike*, most simply means "pond" or "pool" but carries nostalgic and affectionate connotations of old, dear, and quiet. The second, *kawazu*, means "frog." This word was already archaic, and for some four hundred years has been used only in verse, when the more common two-syllable word will not fit.

These are not plain words like those in "The Red Wheelbarrow" by William Carlos Williams or "City" by Langston Hughes. In Japanese, these words are charged with poetic history, and each evokes not only the literature read by Bashō but the tension of a man who learned to love nature, though he lived in a tightly organized society on the edge of the ancient civilizations of China and the Far East.

The surprise in these lines about a frog is that it is silent. The only noise mentioned is the sound of water.

## Commentary

The haiku form can be composed recognizably in most languages. Children and beginners can quickly learn how to write a decently readable haiku verse more easily than a sonnet or a *ruba'i* quatrain. The challenge is to write a great one. "Great haiku cuts both ways, sometimes witty or sarcastic," according to Sam Hamill. "Haiku written in American English and attempting to borrow traditional Japanese literacy devices usually ends up smelling of the bric-a-brac shop, all fragmentary dust and mold or cheap glitter coating the ordinary, or worse, the merely cute or contrived."[1]

This frog poem was composed in early 1686. It apparently became instantly famous, as "by April, the poets of Edo gathered at the Bashō Hut for a haikai no renga contest on the subject of frogs that seems to have been a tribute to Bashō's hokku, which was placed at the top of the compilation."[2]

A 1983 book on translations of Japanese poetry into English collected in one chapter a hundred translations of Bashō's frog verse—eighty-three arranged in chronological order from the end of the nineteenth century, and more than two dozen by modern poets. "There are gems and howlers throughout the entire chapter," reported one reviewer, adding, "one can only feel a kind of awe at the existence of so many wildly different versions … [and] the powerful hold of Bashō's little frog on the imagination of aficionados of Japanese literature."[3]

# Second Poem

From time to time
The clouds give rest
To the moon beholders

(translated by R. H. Blyth)


Clouds—
a chance to dodge
moonviewing.

(translated by Lucien Stryk)


Glorious the moon
therefore our thanks, dark clouds
come to rest our necks.

(translated by Peter Beilenson)

*Third Poem*

*Delight, then sorrow,*
*aboard the cormorant*
*fishing boat*

## Critical Response To Bashō

Soji considers Bashō to be "the poet without whom haiku might never have evolved beyond an after-dinner game for wealthy merchants, samurai and members of the imperial court."[4] The great age of haiku lasted about a century, but Bashō is still venerated in Japan and around the world as one of its masters. The Shinto bureaucracy deified Bashō in 1793, and it was then considered blasphemous to criticize Bashō's verse. But in the late nineteenth century, Masaoka Shiki presented candid and bold objections to Bashō's style, as well as making Bashō's poems more accessible to the ordinary Japanese readers as well as intellectuals. To this day, thousands of Japanese and poets around the world still compose haiku for many magazines and books.

"The precise and concise nature of haiku influenced the early 20th-century Anglo-American poetic movement known as imagism," according to Sam Hamill. "In addition to being the supreme artist of haiku and renga, Bashō wrote haibun, brief prose-and-poetry travelogues … that are absolutely nonpareil in the literature of the world."[5]

## For Further Reading

Japanese masters of the haiku include Buson, Issa, and Masaoka Shiki. Jeong Cheol was a sixteenth-century poet in Korea, and Kim Myong-sun a modern pioneer of Korean women's writing.

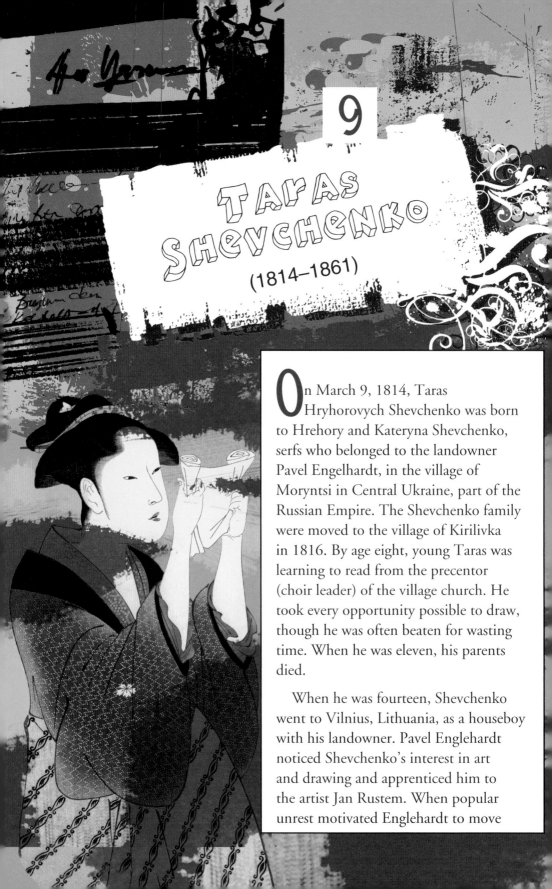

# TARAS SHEVCHENKO
## (1814–1861)

On March 9, 1814, Taras Hryhorovych Shevchenko was born to Hrehory and Kateryna Shevchenko, serfs who belonged to the landowner Pavel Engelhardt, in the village of Moryntsi in Central Ukraine, part of the Russian Empire. The Shevchenko family were moved to the village of Kirilivka in 1816. By age eight, young Taras was learning to read from the precentor (choir leader) of the village church. He took every opportunity possible to draw, though he was often beaten for wasting time. When he was eleven, his parents died.

When he was fourteen, Shevchenko went to Vilnius, Lithuania, as a houseboy with his landowner. Pavel Englehardt noticed Shevchenko's interest in art and drawing and apprenticed him to the artist Jan Rustem. When popular unrest motivated Englehardt to move

A statue of Taras Shevchenko is part of a monument to the poet in Ukraine.

his entourage to Saint Petersburg in 1831, he apprenticed Shevchenko to Vasiliy Shiriaev for four years. Shevchenko also began writing poetry, but did not publish.

In Saint Petersburg, Shevchenko met Ivan Soshenko, a Ukrainian artist, and through him other Ukrainian and Russian painters. One of them, Karl Briullov, donated his portrait of Russian poet Vasily Zhukovsky as a prize in a lottery; the 2,500 rubles raised went to buy Shevchenko's freedom on May 5, 1838. At the age of twenty-four, Shevchenko was no longer a serf.

Accepted that year as a student in the Academy of Arts, in Briullov's workshop, he became a resident student. Three times at the annual examinations, Shevchenko was awarded a silver medal for his paintings. His first collection of poetry, *Kobzar,* was published in 1840, followed

# FACTS

## Creativity in Exile

The czar's ban on Shevchenko's creative work was enforced only during some periods of his exile. One officer allowed him to be the staff artist on the Butakov expedition to explore the Aral Sea, and again during another expedition in Kazakhstan that discovered several coalfields in the Kara-Tau hills. But after that, he was caught writing poems in small notebooks he kept hidden in his boot. For that offense, he was banished still further to Novopetrovsk Fortress (today called Fort Shevchenko) on the eastern shore of the Caspian Sea. Still, "in his 'prison without doors,' as he himself called it, Shevchenko in the period of ten years created the greater part of his wonderful works,"[1] poetry, several portraits, and watercolor landscape paintings.

yearly by an epic poem, a ballad, and two dramas. Completing his studies in 1845, he was granted the title of artist by the academy.

Shevchenko traveled home to Ukraine in 1843, 1845, and 1846. Deeply impressed by the difficult conditions under which his serf siblings, relatives, and countrymen lived, he made *Picturesque Ukraine,* an album of drawings showing cultural monuments and historical ruins. While in Kiev, he was appointed to the Archaeological Commission. He became friends with prominent Ukrainian intellectuals and the noble Repnin family. But his friendship with the Brotherhood of Saints Cyril and Methodius, a political society dedicated to liberalization of the Russian Empire as a federation of Slavic nations, and freeing the serfs without revolutionary action, had serious consequences.

When Shevchenko and the other members were denounced and arrested in 1847, his poem "The Dream" was found during the search. As it criticized imperial rule, it was considered extremely inflammatory. Shevchenko's punishment was more severe than that for the other members of the society. Without a trial, he was imprisoned in Saint Petersburg, interrogated, and then sentenced to twenty-five years of military service in exile at the garrison at Orsk. His sentence was confirmed by Czar Nicholas I, who handwrote the addition that he was to be under the strictest surveillance, without a right to write or paint.

For ten years, Private Shevchenko served as a soldier-guard and traveled on assignment. Only after his friends made many appeals was Shevchenko able to receive a pardon and return from exile in 1857. At first, he was ordered to live in Nizhniy Novgorod, and two years later he was given permission to move to Ukraine. Before he could buy a plot of land and settle down, Shevchenko was arrested on a charge of blasphemy. Released, he was sent to Saint Petersburg.

There he edited his works and created new poetry, paintings, and engravings. Ill health troubled him, and he died March 10, 1861. Seven days later, the emancipation of the serfs by Czar Alexander II was announced. Shevchenko was buried first in Saint Petersburg, but his friends had his remains brought to his homeland. A memorial museum now stands at his grave near Kaniv.

# I Was Thirteen

(translated by John Weir, 1961)

I was thirteen. I herded lambs
Beyond the village on the lea.
The magic of the sun, perhaps,
Or what was it affected me?
I felt with joy all overcome,
As though with God ...
The time for lunch had long passed by,
And still among the weeds I lay
And prayed to God ... I know not why
It was so pleasant then to pray
For me, an orphan peasant boy,
Or why such bliss so filled me there?
The sky seemed bright, the village fair,
The very lambs seemed to rejoice!
The sun's rays warmed but did not sear!
But not for long the sun stayed kind,
Not long in bliss I prayed ...
It turned into a ball of fire
And set the world ablaze.
As though just wakened up, I gaze:
The hamlet's drab and poor,
And God's blue heavens—even they
Are glorious no more.
I look upon the lambs I tend—
Those lambs are not my own!
I eye the hut wherein I dwell—
I do not have a home!
God gave me nothing, naught at all ...

*I bowed my head and wept*
*Such bitter tears … And then a lass*
*Who had been sorting hemp*
*Not far from there, down by the path,*
*Heard my lament and came*
*Across the field to comfort me;*
*She spoke a soothing phrase*
*And gently dried my weeping eyes*
*And kissed my tear-wet face …*
*It was as though the sun had smiled,*
*As though all things on earth were mine,*
*My own … the orchards, fields and groves!…*
*And, laughing merrily the while,*
*The master's lambs to drink we drove.*

*Oh, how disgusting!… Yet, when I*
*Recall those days, my heart is sore*
*That there my brief life's span the Lord*
*Did not grant me to live and die.*
*There, plowing, I'd have passed away,*
*With ignorance my life-long lot,*
*I'd not an outcast be today,*
*I'd not be cursing Man and God!…*

## Summary and Explication

The narrator tells of when he was young and had a joyous moment feeling united with God and a fair world, but then realized that he lived in miserable poverty and owned nothing. His distress brought a girl who comforted him, and he felt as though all things on earth were his. Then he and the girl were happy, bringing their master's lambs to water.

He is disgusted that he could ever have been so happy as a serf. But he is also sad now that he did not live and die there in ignorance. If so, he would not be an outcast now, cursing his fellow man and his creator.

## Poetic Techniques

By writing of his boyhood working as a shepherd, Shevchenko is showing that not only the deeds of heroes and the pastimes of nobles are worthy of poetry.

## Themes

At thirteen, a Jewish boy is expected to announce to his community "Today I am a man" at his Bar Mitzvah. Shevchenko was not a Jew, but coming-of-age ceremonies are common to many cultures around the world. Both boys and girls are encouraged by their community to acknowledge the transition.

Each child comes to the age of reason in his or her own time, whether or not his society formally recognizes or celebrates that transition from a childhood innocence to a status in which they are expected to take on some or all of the responsibilities of an adult. Shevchenko is writing of this moment, and how after the girl's comforting he was still content as a peasant under a master. It seems that he has had a second epiphany, sometime later, in which he became disgusted that he was content with his lot. Yet he also regrets that his fate took him away from life in that village, a regret the French call "nostalgie de la boue": yearning for the mud, or an attraction to what is crude or degrading.

# Commentary

This poem was composed in 1847 while the poet was a prisoner in Orsk Fortress. It was translated by John Weir in 1961, in Toronto, Ontario, in Canada, where there is a substantial population of Ukrainian immigrants and their descendants. It is understandable that while in prison, Shevchenko would return in memory to scenes from his youth, particularly moments where he was happy or comforted. It is also understandable that Ukrainians far from their native land would find that Shevchenko's poems, like this one, could help them return in memory to their own homeland.

The "lass" of the poem was Oksana Kovalenko, a young woman who grew up with Shevchenko. He dedicated his "Poem to Oksana" to her, written in May 1847 while he was in prison in the Saint Petersburg Citadel.

As the character Enkidu in the epic of *Gilgamesh* was tamed and embraced and brought to the great city of Uruk by the woman Shamhat, so the narrator of this poem is calmed and kissed and brought to contentment in his home village by a girl. And as Enkidu later briefly rues the day Shamhat brought him to the city, unhappy with the turn his life has taken, so the narrator is unhappy with the turn his life has taken, at the ending of this poem.

# Don't Wed

(translated by John Weir, 1961)

*Don't wed a wealthy woman, friend,*
*She'll drive you from the house.*
*Don't wed a poor one either, friend,*
*Dull care will be your spouse.*
*Get hitched to carefree Cossack life*
*And share a Cossack fate:*
*If it be rags, let it be rags—*
*What comes, that's what you take.*
*Then you'll have nobody to nag*
*Or try to cheer you up,*
*To fuss and fret and question you*
*What ails you and what's up.*
*When two misfortune share, they say,*
*It's easier to weep.*
*Not so: it's easier to cry*
*When no-one's there to see.*

## Critical Response To Shevchenko

As a major contribution to the growth of Ukrainian nationalism, Shevchenko's poetry influenced Ukrainian intellectuals from his youth to the present day. "His poetry [has] been published in thousands of volumes, including translations into the major world languages."[2] His writings were the foundation of modern Ukrainian literature and even formalized the written language.

In Soviet times, Shevchenko was presented as an anti-Czarist writing in Russian as well, speaking out against the plight of the serfs in the class struggle within the Russian Empire. He was honored by his fellow citizens in Ukraine and also those who had emigrated to other countries, as speaking with their voice of their experiences. He created over a thousand portraits and landscapes, pioneered the art of etching in the Russian Empire, and spoke out in favor of human rights and women's rights and freedom of religion.

## Suggested Further Reading

Readers who admire Shevchenko can look to those who strongly influenced him: Pushkin, the satirist Saltykov-Shchredrin, and Nikolai Gogol; and to modern writers of Eastern European descent, such as Myrna Kostash.

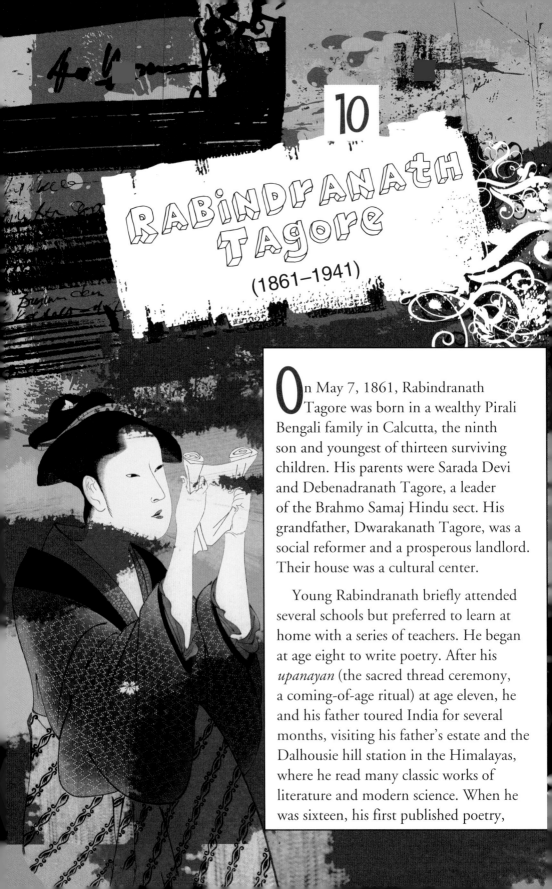

# RABINDRANATH Tagore

## (1861–1941)

On May 7, 1861, Rabindranath Tagore was born in a wealthy Pirali Bengali family in Calcutta, the ninth son and youngest of thirteen surviving children. His parents were Sarada Devi and Debenadranath Tagore, a leader of the Brahmo Samaj Hindu sect. His grandfather, Dwarakanath Tagore, was a social reformer and a prosperous landlord. Their house was a cultural center.

Young Rabindranath briefly attended several schools but preferred to learn at home with a series of teachers. He began at age eight to write poetry. After his *upanayan* (the sacred thread ceremony, a coming-of-age ritual) at age eleven, he and his father toured India for several months, visiting his father's estate and the Dalhousie hill station in the Himalayas, where he read many classic works of literature and modern science. When he was sixteen, his first published poetry,

Rabindranath Tagore

short stories, and dramas began appearing under a pseudonym. Two magazines published by his household regularly used his contributions, including his translation of Shakespeare's *Macbeth* into Bengali verse.

His first book of poems was published in 1878, just before he was sent to England at age seventeen with his brother for formal schooling. Tagore studied law at University College in London but returned to Bengal without a degree in 1880. Home schooling and travels had made him both a pragmatist and a nonconformist.

In 1883, when he was twenty-two, Tagore married Bhabatarini Devi, who was twelve years younger than he. Her name was later changed to Mrinalini Devi. Tagore was devoted to her and their five children, two of whom died in childhood. In 1890, he began managing the family estates

# FACTS

## Tagore's Poetry in English

Tagore made a second visit to England in 1912. On the long sea voyage, he began translating his latest poems into English in a little notebook, for something to do. The notebook was left by his son in a briefcase on the London subway. Luckily, the briefcase was recovered. When the painter Rothenstein, Tagore's lone friend in England, heard of the translation, he persuaded Tagore to let him have the notebook.

Rothenstein was able to convince another friend, the poet W. B. Yeats, to read the notebook. Enthralled with the poetry of *Gitanjali (Song Offerings)*, Yeats arranged for publication and wrote the introduction. With the book's release in September 1912, Tagore was an overnight international success at age fifty-one, in London literary circles and later throughout the world on speaking tours.

in what is now Bangladesh; this kept Tagore aware of the lives of the common people and increased his interest in social reforms. He founded a school in 1901, a year before his wife died, and the school was a great comfort to him in his grief. During this time, Tagore wrote many poems and stories in Bengali, to great acclaim. He modernized Bengali art by composing in modern forms such as short stories as well as classical Indian forms. In 1913, he was the first Indian writer to be awarded the Nobel Prize for Literature.

As recognition of his literary achievements, Tagore was knighted in 1915. At that time, India was still under British rule. But he repudiated his knighthood in 1919 to protest the massacre at Jalianwalabag, in the Punjab province. (In this tragic event, British troops fired upon a group of Indians, peaceably assembled for a festival. Estimates are that more than a thousand people—men, women, and children—were killed.)

With agricultural economist Leonard Emhirst in 1921, Tagore expanded his school into Viswabharati University (an institute for rural reconstruction), endowing it with all the royalties from his books and the prize money from his 1913 Nobel Prize for Literature. Tagore toured many countries in the 1920s, giving talks and raising funds for Viswabharati. Fund-raising was not very fruitful in the United States, because Tagore was seen as anti-British and pro-German. In fact, he was pro-Indian; he was a devoted friend of Gandhi and Nehru. "He was opposed to nationalism and militarism as a matter of principle," according to an authorized biography, "and instead promoted spiritual values and the creation of a new world culture founded in multi-culturalism, diversity and tolerance."[1]

Oxford University awarded an honorary doctorate of literature to Tagore in 1940, during the last year of his life. On August 7, 1941, Tagore died in the family home where he was born.

# Song Unsung

(translated by the author)

*The song that I came to sing remains unsung to this day.*
*I have spent my days in stringing and in unstringing my*
*    instrument.*
*The time has not come true, the words have not been*
*    rightly set;*
*only there is the agony of wishing in my heart.*
*The blossom has not opened; only the wind is sighing by.*
*I have not seen his face, nor have I listened to his voice;*
*only I have heard his gentle footsteps from the road before*
*    my house.*
*The livelong day has passed in spreading his seat on the*
*    floor;*
*but the lamp has not been lit and I cannot ask him into*
*    my house.*

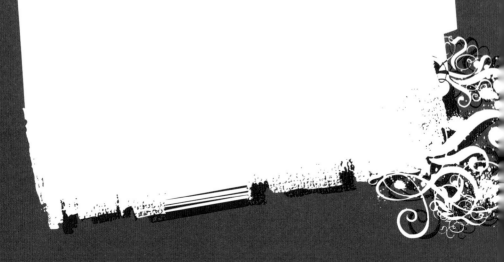

## Summary and Explication

The narrator speaks of preparing for something without experiencing
the actual event. The tension of anticipation has not been fulfilled by the
arrival and entry of the Visitor into the narrator's house.

## Poetic Techniques

Tagore has translated his poem into a plainspoken style rather than one
that is formally poetic. Every line is a complete phrase or sentence, with
subject/verb/object word order, all on a single line without enjambment,
which would place the subject and object of a verb on separate lines. This
avoidance of enjambment brings immediacy and a natural feeling to these
lines, without tension.

It is hinted by the line "The blossom has not opened; only the wind
is sighing by" that the visitor is the narrator's beloved, and intimacy was
desired, but that wish has been frustrated.

## Themes

This poem touches on the same themes as the *Song of Solomon*, when
the beloved is at the door, as well as the biblical parable about the wise
and the foolish virgins who are waiting with their lamps to light the way
for the Bridegroom.

As well, the narrator's unfulfilled preparations are a metaphor for
artistic creation. Tagore is writing here of what it is like to experience a
creative impasse, or "writer's block." One can be as prepared as possible
to compose, one can be making and discarding notes, one can be ready to
create a song, but making oneself ready for inspiration does not guarantee
that inspiration will come. Inspiration is a mystery.

## Commentary

The translation of this poem from Bengali into English was done by
Tagore himself, as he translated most of his own works gradually during

his long life. Readers may not be aware how much effect a translation can have upon the original concepts of a poem, let alone more subtle intentions. The Italians have a saying: *tradutore, traditore,* which means, the *translator is a traitor.*

This poem is an ironic work, for though the poet may be writing about his own experiences and feelings of not making a song, there were many occasions on which he did set the words rightly and sing the song he came to sing. Or at least, he set some words rightly in the opinions of many readers, and he sang many songs that worked for those occasions, whether or not he ever wrote the poems for which he was in an agony of wishing.

The closing comment that "the lamp has not been lit" is an image that, for most North Americans, will work better if one visualizes a cartoon character with a light bulb drawn over its head, as inspiration occurs.

# Colored Toys

(translated by the author)

When I bring to you colored toys, my child,
I understand why there is such a play of colors on
   clouds, on water,
and why flowers are painted in tints
—when I give colored toys to you, my child.

When I sing to make you dance
I truly know why there is music in leaves,
and why waves send their chorus of voices to the heart
   of the listening earth
—when I sing to make you dance.

When I bring sweet things to your greedy hands
I know why there is honey in the cup of the flowers
and why fruits are secretly filled with sweet juice
—when I bring sweet things to your greedy hands.

When I kiss your face to make you smile, my darling,
I surely understand what pleasure streams from the sky
   in morning light,
and what delight that is which the summer breeze
   brings to my body
—when I kiss you to make you smile.

# The Prisoner
(translated by the author)

*"Prisoner, tell me, who was it that bound you?"*

*"It was my master," said the prisoner.*
*"I thought I could outdo everybody in the world in wealth*
*    and power,*
*and I amassed in my own treasure-house the money due to*
*    my king.*
*When sleep overcame me I lay upon the bed that was for*
*    my lord,*
*and on waking up I found I was a prisoner in my own*
*    treasure-house."*

*"Prisoner, tell me, who was it that wrought this*
*    unbreakable chain?"*

*"It was I," said the prisoner, "Who forged this chain very*
*    carefully.*
*I thought my invincible power would hold the world captive*
*leaving me in a freedom undisturbed.*
*Thus night and day I worked at the chain*
*with huge fires and cruel hard strokes.*
*When at last the work was done*
*and the links were complete and unbreakable,*
*I found that it held me in its grip."*

## Critical Response To Tagore

"Tagore had early success as a writer in his native Bengal," says scholar Horst Frenz. "For the world he became the voice of India's spiritual heritage; and for India, especially for Bengal, he became a great living institution."[2] He is considered by many to be the ambassador of Indian culture to the rest of the world, and their most prominent cultural figure of modern times.

The scholarly goals Tagore sought all his life gave him the confidence to hold his own in a debate with Einstein and strengthened his lasting friendship with Gandhi. But his intent to share his learning and insistence on making education available to others made him a peer to other founders of universities, such as Leland Stanford and Ezra Cornell in the United States.

Tagore composed the national anthems of India and of Bangladesh; on both occasions, he was the natural choice as an activist poet and author, the living voice of his people. His songs are still sung by Bengalis and are popularly known as *Rabindrasangeet.*

## Suggested Further Reading

Tagore wrote more than fifty books of poetry, of which *Gitanjali (Song Offerings)* is among the most famous and most popular with Western readers. Readers looking for other works by Indian writers can look to Khalil Gibran, Shani Mootoo, Ramabai Espinet, and Sankha Ghosh, among many others.

# ANNA AKHMATOVA

## (1889–1966)

Anna Akhmatova was the pseudonym of Anna Andreevna Gorenko, born June 23, 1889, at Boshoy Fontan in Odessa, Ukraine. She was educated at Tsarskoye Selo, near Saint Petersburg, and at Kiev. Her childhood does not appear to have been a happy one, as her parents separated in 1905. At the age of eleven, inspired by reading Pushkin, Racine, and Baratynsky, young Anna began writing poetry. Her father did not want his respectable, noble family name tarred with decadent poetry, so she used the name of her Tatar grandmother as a pen name.

In 1910, Akhmatova married Nikolai Gumilyov, cofounder of the Guild of Poets, a literary movement advocating craftsmanship, later called Acmeism. Akhmatova impressed the literary circles in Saint Petersburg with her artistic integrity and aristocratic manners. Her first collection of poems was published in

A painting of Anna Akhmatova by N. I. Altman

1912, the year her son, Lev, was born. Lev was later to become a famous historian. By 1914, when her second collection was published, thousands of Russian women were writing poems in her honor as the events of the Russian Revolution were taking place.

But her husband, Gumilyov, did not take her poems seriously; he left her after their honeymoon to tour in Africa and then fought in the First World War. They were divorced in 1918. Gumilov was later arrested and executed in 1921 on trumped-up charges of being part of a monarchist conspiracy.

Akhmatova married a distinguished Assyriologist Vladimir Shileiko, but they separated in 1920 and in 1928 were divorced.

After 1922, Akhmatova was condemned by the Russian Communist government as a bourgeois element (a middle-class person who has a bad influence on workers). Publication of her poetry was banned from 1925 to 1940. All her literary friends were similarly repressed, imprisoned, or

# FACTS

## Akhmatova and Stalin

Sir Isaiah Berlin reported that when they met again in Oxford in 1965, Akhmatova told him that Stalin was enraged because she had allowed Berlin to visit her. "So our nun now received visits from foreign spies," Stalin is alleged to have remarked.... All members of foreign missions were spies to Stalin. Of course, she said, the old man was by then ... in the grip of pathological paranoia. In Oxford she told me that she was convinced that Stalin's fury, which we had raised, had unleashed the Cold War–that she and I had changed the history of mankind.[1]

forced to emigrate. She earned her living by writing essays for scholarly journals, memoirs, and translations of Rabindranath Tagore, Victor Hugo, and the Italian scholar Giacomo Leopardi.

Akhmatova's third husband, Nikolai Punin, and her son, Lev, were arrested in 1935, as were several friends. Lev was released when his mother wrote to Stalin, but he was arrested again in 1938. He served in the air force on his release.

Akhmatova was allowed to publish a new collection of poems in 1940, and during the Second World War, her patriotic poems appeared on the front page of *Pravda*, the state newspaper. But in 1946, visits from the British political philosopher Sir Isaiah Berlin put her in disgrace. Her poems were banned from publication. Her son, Lev, was arrested again in 1949, and spent fifteen years in a Siberian gulag. Akhmatova was able to secure his release only by writing several poems praising Stalin. Her husband, Punin, died in a Siberian camp in the 1950s.

Still officially banned from publication in the Soviet Union, Akhmatova continued to compose. When she went out, the KGB—the Soviet secret police—searched her modest home and confiscated anything written. Rarely, a friend would visit, and she would write out a poem from memory while making tea. The friend would commit the poem to memory and burn it, while maintaining a conversation for the benefit of the KGB's listening devices. Her poems circulated in *samizdat* (illegal small-press publications) and by word of mouth as a symbol of suppressed Russian heritage.

Akhmatova's official rehabilitation after Stalin's death in 1953 was a gradual process that censored her work for years but eventually gave her permission from the government to publish. She moved from the Fontanka Embankment to a dacha (country home) in Komorovo that was visited by young Russian poets and in 1962 by Robert Frost. It was only in 1964 that new collections of her verse were published. The next year, she was allowed to visit Sicily to accept the Taormina Prize and England to receive an honorary doctorate from Oxford University, traveling with her lifelong friend Lydia Korneievna Chukovskaya. Akhmatova died on March 5, 1966.

*Excerpt from*

# Lot's Wife

(translated by Yevgeny Bonver)

*Holy Lot was a-going behind God's angel,*
*He seemed huge and bright on a hill, huge and black.*
*But the heart of his wife whispered stronger and stranger:*
*"It's not very late, you have time to look back*
*At these rose turrets of your native Sodom,*
*The square where you sang, and the yard where you span,*
*The windows looking from your cozy home*
*Where you bore children for your dear man."*
*She looked—and her eyes were instantly bound*
*By pain—they couldn't see any more at all:*
*Her fleet feet grew into the stony ground,*
*Her body turned into a pillar of salt.*

*Who'll mourn her as one of Lot's family members?*
*Doesn't she seem the smallest of losses to us?*
*But deep in my heart I will always remember*
*One who gave her life up for one single glance.*

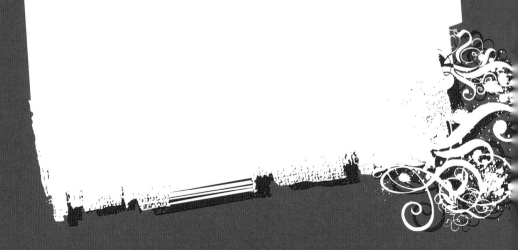

## Summary and Explication

In the book of Genesis, God intended to destroy the city of Sodom because the people were sinful. Lot and his family hosted two visiting angels, who warned them to flee the city and not look back. But Lot's wife looked back and was turned into a pillar of salt.

## Poetic Techniques

It is a poetic tradition, as in the *glosas* written in Spain, to take a brief excerpt from an earlier work by another poet and expand upon it. Often the style and mood is kept the same as in the original, expanding the original vision. But in the best of glosas, and here in this poem, the poet begins with the brief excerpt and, without contradicting it in any way, develops and fulfills the moment in ways that were not manifest in the original verse. Ahkmatova has taken as her starting text sixteen words about a character who was written into the Sodom story only to die like a spear-carrier in an epic or a red-shirted security officer on *Star Trek*. In her expansion, she has given Lot's wife a past, as well as feelings and wishes and memories like a real person.

## Themes

The foreign setting for this poem is made overt by the phrase "rose turrets" to describe the little towers on roofs in the city of Sodom. Were they rosy from catching the warm light of sunrise and sunset in the hot country near Palestine? Or the rock used for building may have been red, as in the ruins of Petra in modern Israel. The poet and her audience lived in a continent where building stone was gray granite or cream-colored limestone, and at a northern latitude where sunlight was thin and warmed only to yellow.

The transition of Lot's wife into a pillar of salt is described here more fully than in *Genesis*. Ahkmatova makes the change seem more like the transformations of Myrrha fleeing her fate and the other women fleeing attentions of various gods in Ovid's *Metamorphoses* than like a momentary thunderbolt.

## Commentary

Akhmatova's early poems usually concerned a poignant, ambivalent moment in the relationship between a man and woman. These poems were frequently imitated, and later Vladimir Nabokov wrote parodies. The death of Lot's wife was certainly both poignant, as nothing of her remained nor was depicted in the original story, not even her name; and it was ambivalent as she followed her man out of the city but lingered to look back. Was she regretting leaving her home, or was she bidding it good riddance? Ahkmatova suggests that she was saying good-bye.

She also suggests in the second line that Lot's wife regarded her husband much as they both did the angel. When the poet writes: "He seemed huge and bright on a hill, huge and black," was the "He" the angel, standing huge and bright on a hill that was huge and black? Or was the "He" her husband, larger than she, his form looking bright against the huge angel beyond him who loomed large and dark? By putting the word "He" at the beginning of the line, Ahkmatova and her translator are carefully not specifying whether "he" refers to the angel or the husband. The conflation here of husband and God's messenger is deliberate and effective.

## I Was Born In the Right Time ...

(translated by Yevgeny Bonver)

*1913*

*I was born in the right time, in whole,*
*Only this time is one that is blessed,*
*But great God did not let my poor soul*
*Live without deceit on this earth.*

*And therefore, it's dark in my house,*
*And therefore, all of my friends,*
*Like sad birds, in the evening aroused,*
*Sing of love, that was never on land.*

*Excerpt from*

# Requiem

(translated by Tanya Karshtedt)

*Instead of a Preface*

*In the awful days of the Yezhovschina I passed
seventeen months in the outer waiting line of the
prison visitors in Leningrad. Once, somebody
'identified' me there. Then a woman, standing
behind me in the line, which, of course, never
heard my name, waked up from the torpor, typical
for us all there, and asked me, whispering into my
ear (all spoke only in a whisper there):
"And can you describe this?"
And I answered:
"Yes, I can."
Then the weak similarity of a smile glided over
that, what had once been her face.
April 1, 1957; Leningrad*

## Critical Response

Akhmatova has been called "one of the greatest Russian poets of the
twentieth century, who became a legend in her own time as a poet
and symbol of artistic integrity. Akhmatova's work is characterized by
precision, clarity, and economy."[2]

Clive James wrote: "Akhmatova was the embodiment of the Russian
liberal heritage that the authoritarians felt bound to go on threatening long
after it had surrendered.... [W]hen a poet becomes better known than her
poems, it usually means that she is being sacrificed, for extraneous reasons,
on the altar of her own glory. In Akhmatova's case, the extraneous reasons
were political."[3] It was only after the collapse of the Soviet Union that

*Requiem*, her greatest cycle of poems, was published in her homeland on the hundredth anniversary of her birth.

## Suggested Further Reading

Ahkmatova's literary influences included Innokentky Annensky, Aleksandr Pushkin, and Vyacheslav Ivanov. Her lifelong friend and biographer, Lydia Korneievna Chukovskaya, was an impressive activist writer. Also, a familiarity with the Russian Revolution and events of World War I and II will make it easier for North American readers to understand the works of poets of Russia, Ukraine, and Eastern Europe.

# Federico García Lorca

## (1898–1936)

In the village of Fuente Vaqueros on the banks of the Genil River, a few miles from Granada in Spain, Federico García Lorca was born on June 5, 1898. His mother, Vicenta Lorca Romero, had been a schoolteacher before becoming the second wife of a prosperous farmer, Federico García Rodriguez. A precocious child, young García Lorca did not excel at school; but when the family moved to Granada in 1909, he became involved in local artistic circles in the Spanish province of Andalusia.

At the University of Granada, Lorca studied law and music and wrote his first book, a travelogue published in 1918. Friendships he made at Granada's Arts Club were helpful when he entered the University of Madrid in 1919, living at the student residences, which were the intellectual center of the city. From his recitations, Lorca developed a reputation

Federico García Lorca

as a poet, even before his first collection of fablelike poems was published in 1921. The writers Pablo Neruda and Juan Ramón Jiménez were his friends; he also collaborated with the composer Manuel de Falla in the 1920s, playing guitar and piano.

Music had a profound effect upon Lorca's literary career, particularly in 1922 when he attended the folk music festival Fiesta de Cante Jondo and found inspiration for his poetry in the traditions of folk and gypsy music. Old ballads and mythology were the core of two of his books, which established Lorca as the premier poet of Andalusia and its gypsy subculture.

With the completion of his law degree in 1923, Lorca left the university. At this time, he met Salvador Dalí, who was deeply impressed by Lorca. Together, Dalí and Lorca worked with the film director Louis Buñuel on many productions, gaining fame and notoriety. Lorca suffered from increasing depression, made worse by feeling trapped between maintaining in public the persona of the successful author, and the tortured self, which he could only acknowledge in private. The famous short film *Un Chien Andalou* (1928) by Buñuel and Dalí offended Lorca, as he assumed the film was about him.

Aware that his friendships with Dalí and with sculptor Emilio Aladrén were collapsing, Lorca's family arranged for him to tour the United States between 1929 and 1930. Lorca lived for a time in New York City, studying at Columbia University. The culture shock he suffered was considerable, as he did not speak English, but even so, he was enthusiastic about American theater when writing letters home. In his posthumously published book, *Poet in New York* (1940), he praised the poetry of Walt Whitman, but it was clear that his mood was becoming suicidal. Condemning the city as frightening and corrupted, Lorca fled to Havana in search of the harmony of a more primitive life.

He returned to Spain by 1931, where he led the traveling theatrical company La Barraca, bringing dramas and classical plays to the provinces. At the height of his powers, and less troubled by depression, Lorca continued to write and to lecture about writing.

When the Spanish Civil War began in 1936, Lorca was considered an enemy by the right-wing forces for performing poetic dramas for the common people. Though he hid from the soldiers, he was eventually found and taken from a government building by guards and Falangist members of the "Black Squad." There was no trial before Lorca was shot in an olive grove in Granada on August 19, and buried in a grave that he had been made to dig. Some sources report that he had to be finished off by a *coup de grâce* [a bullet to the head]. According to Lorca's biographer Ian Gibson, "Among the assassins … was Juan Luis Trescastro … who boasted later that morning in Granada that he had just helped to shoot Lorca."[1] The last words Lorca wrote were a note on behalf of a member of the "Black Squad"—probably written under duress. The note read simply: "Father, please give this man a donation of 1000 pesetas for the Army." His father, Federico García Rodriguez, carried the note in his wallet for the rest of his life.

# FACTS

## The Spanish Civil War

In Spain, increasing violence between the government and militant Fascists came to a head on July 18, 1936, when generals Francisco Franco and Yoldi Orgasz seized control of the Canary Islands, beginning a civil war that would last three years. International tensions throughout Europe increased during this time, and the Spanish Civil War was largely seen as a proxy war between the Soviet Union supporting the Republicans and Fascist Italy and Nazi Germany supporting the rebellion. Many journalists covered the war, including Ernest Hemingway, Martha Gellhorn, and George Orwell. When the rebel forces succeeded in overthrowing the Republican government, a dictatorship led by Franco fused all the right-wing parties into his regime.

# Sonnet of the Sweet Complaint

(translated by Robert Pring-Mill)

*Never let me lose the marvel*
*of your statue-like eyes, or the accent*
*the solitary rose of your breath*
*places on my cheek at night.*

*I am afraid of being, on this shore,*
*a branchless trunk, and what I most regret*
*is having no flower, pulp, or clay*
*for the worm of my despair.*

*If you are my hidden treasure,*
*if you are my cross, my dampened pain,*
*if I am a dog and you alone my master,*
*never let me lose what I have gained,*
*and adorn the branches of your river*
*with leaves of my estranged Autumn.*

## Summary and Explication

The narrator is saying to his beloved: Never leave me. I fear I cannot live without you. If you are everything I value, do not let me lose everything. Let me adore you as I face growing older.

## Poetic Techniques

Sonnets are a popular form used by European poets since the Renaissance. Based on sonnets ("little songs") composed by Petrarch and other Italian poets, the fourteen lines of a sonnet are written as first an octet of eight lines, which may be in two verses, followed by a sestet of six lines. Usually, the thought presented in the octet is answered by the thought presented in the sestet. Though a sonnet may have any of several rhyme schemes, usually each line is written in iambic pentameter.

This sonnet is a distinct variation on any of the standard patterns, as there is no end rhyme pattern in the English translation, and the lines, written in iambic tetrameter, have four beats, not five.

Lorca uses a simile ("statue-like eyes") and a series of metaphors, rather than overt descriptions of the beloved, the "you" in the poem.

## Themes

A water theme dominates the poem, in which the beloved is described in watery metaphors, as a shore, as dampened pain, and as a river with branches. Though these words are without gender in English, the thematic association suggests that the beloved may be a woman.

That the narrator is a man is suggested by the second verse's images of the worm and the fear that he will be "a branchless trunk." In this verse, the narrator extends the plant metaphor begun when his beloved's breath is called a "solitary rose." His fear of being dead and immobile as a limbless tree without his beloved, who is fair as a living flower, is one interpretation of the poem. Another interpretation is that the narrator is despairing that he is growing older. Fearing that he will be impotent, he begs not to lose his beloved, who is everything that matters to him.

## commentary

Lorca is able to write of both sexual desire and simple physical intimacy ("your breath / … on my cheek at night") without descending into erotica or mere vulgarity. It shows a careful sensibility, to be expected from a man who tried to keep his own love affairs private.

Lorca's theories on artistic creation were detailed in his lecture "Play and Theory of the Duende," which he gave in Havana and Buenos Aires in 1933. Great art depends upon a vivid awareness of death, as Lorca shows in this "Sonnet of the Sweet Complaint"; connection with a nation's soil is also required, and an acknowledgment that reason has limitations.

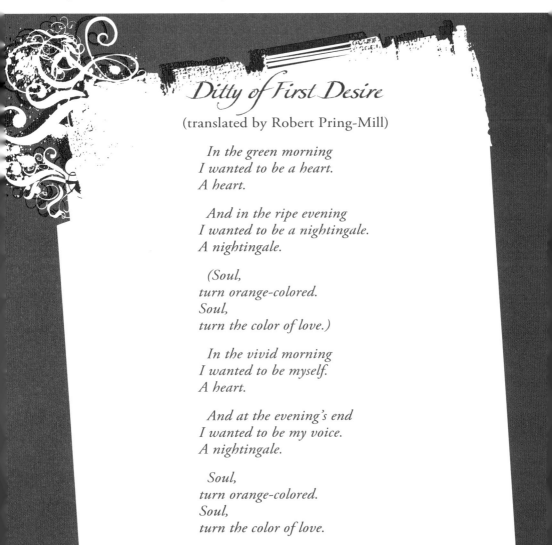

## Ditty of First Desire

(translated by Robert Pring-Mill)

*In the green morning*
*I wanted to be a heart.*
*A heart.*

*And in the ripe evening*
*I wanted to be a nightingale.*
*A nightingale.*

*(Soul,*
*turn orange-colored.*
*Soul,*
*turn the color of love.)*

*In the vivid morning*
*I wanted to be myself.*
*A heart.*

*And at the evening's end*
*I wanted to be my voice.*
*A nightingale.*

*Soul,*
*turn orange-colored.*
*Soul,*
*turn the color of love.*

# The Gypsy and the Wind

(translated by Robert Pring-Mill)

*Playing her parchment moon*
*Precosia comes*
*along a watery path of laurels and crystal lights.*
*The starless silence, fleeing*
*from her rhythmic tambourine,*
*falls where the sea whips and sings,*
*his night filled with silvery swarms.*
*High atop the mountain peaks*
*the sentinels are weeping;*
*they guard the tall white towers*
*of the English consulate.*
*And gypsies of the water*
*for their pleasure erect*
*little castles of conch shells*
*and arbors of greening pine.*

*Playing her parchment moon*
*Precosia comes.*
*The wind sees her and rises,*
*the wind that never slumbers.*
*Naked Saint Christopher swells,*
*watching the girl as he plays*
*with tongues of celestial bells*
*on an invisible bagpipe.*

*Gypsy, let me lift your skirt*
*and have a look at you.*
*Open in my ancient fingers*
*the blue rose of your womb.*

Precosia throws the tambourine
and runs away in terror.
But the virile wind pursues her
with his breathing and burning sword.

The sea darkens and roars,
while the olive trees turn pale.
The flutes of darkness sound,
and a muted gong of the snow.

Precosia, run, Precosia!
Or the green wind will catch you!
Precosia, run, Precosia!
And look how fast he comes!
A satyr of low-born stars
with their long and glistening tongues.

Precosia, filled with fear,
now makes her way to that house
beyond the tall green pines
where the English consul lives.

Alarmed by the anguished cries,
three riflemen come running,
their black capes tightly drawn,
and berets down over their brow.

The Englishman gives the gypsy
a glass of tepid milk
and a shot of Holland gin
which Precosia does not drink.

And while she tells them, weeping,
of her strange adventure,
the wind furiously gnashes
against the slate roof tiles.

## CriTicaL Response To García Lorca

Lorca was arguably the best known of all living Spanish poets by 1928, and a leader of the avant-garde literary movement called the Generation of 27 (for 1927). Robert Pring-Mill wrote:

> His murder by the Nationalists at the start of the Spanish civil war brought sudden international fame, accompanied by an excess of political rhetoric which led a later generation to question his merits. His reputation has recovered.... [He is] one of the two greatest poets Spain has produced this century, and he is certainly Spain's greatest dramatist since the Golden Age. Lorca's technical experimentation (which has affinities with innovators as dissimilar as Pirandello and Brecht) was immensely versatile, and he had a superb sense for stage-effects to reinforce the web of his recurrent imagery.[2]

Lorca is also remembered as a painter, pianist, and composer.

## SuggesTed FurTher Reading

Other members of the Generation of 27 include Luis Gernuda, Jorge Guillen, Pedro Salinas, and Rafael Alberti. Readers looking for the experiences of other writers in the Spanish Civil War can read the works of Langston Hughes, André Malraux, and José Ortega y Gasset.

# PABLO NERUDA

## (1904–1973)

**P**ablo Neruda is the pen name of Neftalí Ricardo Reyes Basoalto. He was born July 12, 1904, in the town of Parral, Chile. His mother was a teacher, and she died shortly after his birth. His father was a railway employee, who moved with his son to the town of Temuco and there married again.

"I grew up in this town, my poetry was born between the hill and the river, it took its voice from the rain, and like the timber, it steeped itself in the forests," the poet said of his youth in Temuco.[1] He was writing poems at age ten, though his father never liked his poetry and actively tried to discourage him from writing. By thirteen, he was contributing articles and poems to the daily paper. He became a contributor to the literary journal *Selva Austral*, using the pen name Pablo Neruda in honor of the Czechoslovak poet Jan

Pablo Neruda

Neruda. At the University of Chile in Santiago, he studied French and education. His first books were published in 1923 and 1924.

Neruda worked as a diplomat, and between 1927 and 1935, he was in charge of a number of honorary consulships at no pay, which brought him to many places in Asia—Burma, Ceylon, Java, Singapore—as well as Buenos Aires, Barcelona, and Madrid. This was a difficult time of poverty and loneliness for him. In Jakarta, he fell in love with and married Maria Antoineta Hagenar. He also wrote many works of poetry, including *Recidencia en la Tierra,* a collection of esoteric surrealistic poems that marked his literary breakthrough in 1933. (Surrealism was an artistic movement expressing subconscious ideas through fantasy imagery.) This was also the year he met Federico García Lorca in Buenos Aires, and they became fast friends.

Affected strongly by the civil war in Spain and by the murder of his friend García Lorca, Neruda joined the Republican movement while he was in Spain. His first marriage ended in 1936; and he met Delia del Carril, who became his second wife. Later, in France, he began working on a new collection of poems, *España en el Corazón* (1937), which had a great impact because it was printed in the middle of the front during the Spanish Civil War.

Appointed the consul for the Spanish emigration in 1939, Neruda lived in Paris before being appointed consul general in Mexico. There he rewrote one of his major works, *Canto General de Chile.* Retitled *Canto General,* it became an epic poem about the historical destiny of the South American continent, its nature, and its people. Published in 1950 in Mexico and underground in Chile, *Canto General* is the central part of Neruda's body of work: a collection of some 250 poems in 15 literary cycles.

Neruda returned to Chile in 1943, and was elected senator of the Republic in 1945 when he joined the Communist Party of Chile. At this time, he also legally changed his name to his pen name. Because he made protests against President Gonzalez Videla's repression of striking miners, Neruda had to live underground for two years until he was able to leave Chile in 1949. He visited the Soviet Union, Hungary, Poland,

and Mexico, where he met Matilde Urrutia, who became his third wife in a marriage that lasted the rest of his life. They returned to Chile in 1952. Much of his published poetry of that time was strongly influenced by his political activities.

The *Obras Completas (Complete Works)* of Neruda totaled 459 pages in 1951; the 1962 edition was 1,925 pages; and in 1968, a two-volume edition held 3,237 pages.

After campaigning for Salvador Allende, who was elected president of Chile in 1969, Neruda was appointed ambassador to France. In 1971, he was awarded the Nobel Prize for Literature. After receiving his prize in Stockholm, Sweden, he returned home, stricken with cancer. He died September 23, 1973, in Santiago, Chile, a few days before his friend Allende died in a coup.

# FACTS

## Inspired by the Incas

Neruda climbed to Machu Picchu during a trip to Peru in 1943. The spectacular ruin of this ancient Inca city inspired him to write one of his finest poems, celebrating pre-Columbian civilization. "Heights of Machu Picchu" became the centerpiece of the revised *Canto General*. He smuggled the manuscript out of the country in his saddlebags when he fled in 1949, crossing the Andes on horseback.

# The White Man's Burden

(translated by Stephen Tapscott)

*Lost in the forest, I broke off a dark twig*
*and lifted its whisper to my thirsty lips:*
*maybe it was the voice of the rain crying,*
*a cracked bell, or a torn heart.*

*Something from far off it seemed*
*deep and secret to me, hidden by the earth,*
*a shout muffled by huge autumns,*
*by the moist half-open darkness of the leaves.*

*Wakening from the dreaming forest there, the hazel-sprig*
*sang under my tongue, its drifting fragrance*
*climbed up through my conscious mind*

*as if suddenly the roots I had left behind*
*cried out to me, the land I had lost with my childhood—*
*and I stopped, wounded by the wandering scent.*

## Summary and Explication

The poet writes of being lost in the forest and breaking off a rain-dark twig to put in his mouth because he is thirsty. The twig's scent and taste has a subtle meaning for him that first seems like a secret being whispered, then becomes clearer. His past is calling to him in memory evoked by the smell.

## Poetic Techniques

This poem is in a sonnet form, though in English it uses none of the familiar rhyme schemes, and the iambic pentameter is so much more irregular than usual for a sonnet that some of the lines have four beats, not five. What confirms that it is still a sonnet in spite of this is that it has fourteen lines, arranged as two verses of four lines followed by two verses of three lines, and also that as in many of Shakespeare's sonnets, the first eight lines "contain a catalogue and the last six turn in quite a different direction."[2]

The only lines that rhyme, the eleventh and twelfth, form a couplet. Usually in sonnets, a rhyming couplet does not occur at this point in the poem. That it does here focuses the attention most particularly on this pair of lines, bringing to the reader's conscious mind a great awareness of the roots the narrator must have left behind.

## Themes

There are many themes briefly evoked in this poem "The White Man's Burden": The narrator is lost, not traveling in the forest; the rain is crying, not washing; the bell (an icon of the Catholic Church) is cracked, not whole; and the heart is torn, not whole, in an idiom that means the narrator is feeling pulled in two directions by different motivations, as well as a reference to Aztec rituals where living hearts were torn from captives' chests.

This twig is from a hazel tree, a European tree, not a South American or an Asian one. It does not matter where in the world stands the wood in which the narrator is lost—he is tasting a tree his white European ancestors would have known well, whether he has stumbled across a wild hazel in Europe or one grown from a seed brought to another continent to grow in foreign soil. He recognizes this twig is of his homeland, and he is tasting his ancestral heritage in this, his "family tree."

## Commentary

What are the roots Neruda has left behind? It's too easy to say that "the land I had lost in childhood" is his homeland in Temuca, Chile, where he grew up, lost when he grew to man's estate and traveled to Europe and Asia. Home would never be the same for one returning from overseas after years of foreign experiences. But even for those who do not travel, home is not the same for an adult who puts away childish behaviors at maturity. And even a child who is wandering in the wild woods in youthful play can be reminded of home left behind by tasting a twig like the trees in the garden at home.

These answers are all true, but for Neruda, the roots left behind are older than these. By being born and having a childhood in Chile, Neruda lost the land of his ancestral roots in Spain. And by being born in a country where most of his fellow citizens are descended from both Spanish stock and the South American peoples, Neruda is neither one nor the other. In the Americas, even those who are not of mixed race are still raised in a mixed society. And that mixing is painful, because little of it came as a result of peaceful traveling—even the wandering scent wounds this poet.

# Love Sonnet XVII

## (translated by William O'Daly)

*I do not love you as if you were a salt rose, or topaz*
*or the arrow of carnations the fire shoots off.*
*I love you as certain dark things are to be loved,*
*in secret, between the shadow and the soul.*

*I love you as the plant that never blooms*
*but carries in itself the light of hidden flowers;*
*thanks to your love a certain solid fragrance,*
*risen from the earth, lives darkly in my body.*

*I love you without knowing how, or when, or from where.*
*I love you straightforwardly, without complexities or pride;*
*So I love you because I know no other way*

*than this: where I does not exist, nor you,*
*so close that your hand on my chest is my hand,*
*so close that your eyes close as I fall asleep.*

# Magellanic Penguin

(translated by Jack Schmitt)

Neither clown nor child nor black
nor white but vertical
and a questioning innocence
dressed in night and snow:
The mother smiles at the sailor,
the fisherman at the astronaut,
but the child child does not smile
when he looks at the bird child,
and from the disorderly ocean
the immaculate passenger
emerges in snowy mourning.

I was without doubt the child bird
there in the cold archipelagoes
when it looked at me with its eyes,
with its ancient ocean eyes:
it had neither arms nor wings
but hard little oars
on its sides:
it was as old as the salt;
the age of moving water,
and it looked at me from its age:
since then I know I do not exist;
I am a worm in the sand.

the reasons for my respect
remained in the sand:
the religious bird
did not need to fly,
did not need to sing,
and through its form was visible
its wild soul bled salt:
as if a vein from the bitter sea
had been broken.

Penguin, static traveler,
deliberate priest of the cold,
I salute your vertical salt
and envy your plumed pride.

## CriTical Response To Neruda

"Neruda was perhaps the most important Latin-American poet of the 20th century, and penned some of the most tender, sensuous, melancholy, erotic and passionate love poetry one will ever read," according to Katharena Eiermann. Like many commentators, she is struck how the despair showing in his early works evolved into a tone reflecting his Socialist commitment. She is not the only critic to identify four major styles in Neruda's writing:

> These four trends correspond to four aspects of Neruda's personality: his passionate love life; the nightmares and depression he experienced while serving as a consul in Asia; his commitment to a political cause; and his ever-present attention to details of daily life, his love of things made or grown by human hands.... Despite the variety of his output as a whole, each of his books has unity of style and purpose.[3]

"The books that help you most are those which make you think the most," Neruda is quoted as saying. "The hardest way of learning is that of easy reading; but a great book that comes from a great thinker is a ship of thought, deep freighted with truth and beauty."[4]

## SuggesTed FurTher Reading

Readers who enjoy Neruda will find much to appreciate in the poetry of P. K. (Patricia) Page, Gioconda Belli, and Ursula K. Le Guin.

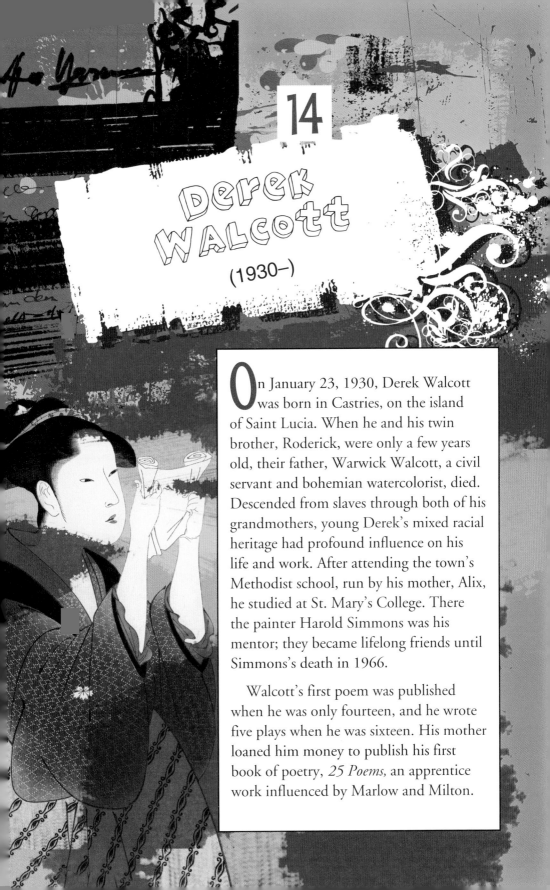

# Derek Walcott

## (1930–)

On January 23, 1930, Derek Walcott was born in Castries, on the island of Saint Lucia. When he and his twin brother, Roderick, were only a few years old, their father, Warwick Walcott, a civil servant and bohemian watercolorist, died. Descended from slaves through both of his grandmothers, young Derek's mixed racial heritage had profound influence on his life and work. After attending the town's Methodist school, run by his mother, Alix, he studied at St. Mary's College. There the painter Harold Simmons was his mentor; they became lifelong friends until Simmons's death in 1966.

Walcott's first poem was published when he was only fourteen, and he wrote five plays when he was sixteen. His mother loaned him money to publish his first book of poetry, *25 Poems,* an apprentice work influenced by Marlow and Milton.

Derek Walcott

He founded the Saint Lucia Arts Guild when he was twenty, producing his play *Henri-Christophe.*

As a young adult, Walcott was deeply interested in the lives of the people of Saint Lucia. This interest grew into a vow he took with a friend who was a painter, in which he promised to write the chronicles of his island home. "Walcott's early play, *Henri-Christophe,* was connected with this intense desire to depict and express the essence of his Caribbean surroundings," says one biographer. "In a later context, Walcott managed with deeper penetration than ever before to give form to a mature attitude to this theme, with a kind of acceptance of the trespasses of his ancestors through the centuries."[1]

After graduating from St. Mary's, Walcott went to Jamaica to continue his studies at the University College of the West Indies at Mona. There

# FACTS

## Walcott's Epic

Walcott's greatest work so far is the epic poem *Omeros* (1990), a gathering of 192 songs written in blank verse, unrhymed iambic pentameter. These poems tell short stories, conversations, flashbacks, monologues, impressions, and more, all showing in minute detail the everyday life of the people and natural elements of the Caribbean world. Homer himself appears in a variety of roles, and other figures are influenced by Homeric characters. Many descendants of slaves in St. Lucia bore classic Greek names. Listening to an argument between two fishermen in his hometown, Walcott could not avoid thinking of characters quarreling in Homer's *Iliad* and *Odyssey.*

he was president of the Mona Dramatic Society and edited the student magazine. He earned a bachelor's degree in 1953.

After graduation, Walcott moved to Trinidad, where he worked from 1953 to 1957 as a teacher in schools on several Caribbean islands before working as a theater and art critic. In 1959, he founded the Trinidad Theatre Workshop, directing it until 1971. Walcott's book of poems *In a Green Night* was his literary breakthrough work.

He married Fay Moston in 1954, and they had a son, but their marriage ended after a few years in 1959. His marriage to his second wife, Margaret Maillard, gave them two daughters before it ended in divorce. Norline Metivier became his third wife in 1976, and that marriage also ended in divorce.

For forty years, Walcott has been the most celebrated West Indian poet and playwright, with some fifteen poetry collections and many stage and radio dramas to his name. He has received many literary awards, including an honorary Doctor of Letters from the University of the West Indies, a MacArthur Foundation "genius" award, a Royal Society of Literature award, an Order of the British Empire, the Queen's Medal for Poetry, and the 1992 Nobel Prize in Literature. Since then, he has created a second master work, *Tiepolo's Hound,* which he illustrated with his own oil and watercolor paintings. In one of the two narrative threads, Walcott appears himself as a poet and failed painter. His third epic poem, *The Prodigal,* was released in 2004.

For decades, Walcott lived in Boston and New York; but in his later years, his living pattern has been to teach creative writing at Boston University every fall and spend the rest of the year in Trinidad and St. Lucia.

Excerpt from
# Crusoe's Island

*Upon this rock the bearded hermit built*
*His Eden:*
*Goats, corn crop, fort, parasol, garden,*
*Bible for Sabbath, all the joys*
*But one*
*Which sent him howling for a human voice.*
*Exiled by a flaming sun*
*The rotting nut, bowled in the surf,*
*Became his own brain rotting from the guilt*
*Of heaven without his kind,*
*Crazed by such paradisal calm*
*The spinal shadow of a palm*
*Built keel and gunwhale in his mind.*

## Summary and Explication

This is a brief description of the life of a castaway on a deserted island. He has everything he needs for a perfect life as humanity was intended to live in Eden, except for someone to talk with. He is going mad without company and wishes to build a boat so he can find other people.

## Poetic Techniques

In this verse in particular, the poet does not rely on fancified images evoking a pretty and delicate kind of poetry. Walcott instead uses simple words and lucid images in plain language. These lines are very easy to read aloud in a natural voice.

Without a regular rhyme scheme, these mostly iambic phrases are constructed as sentences broken up for emphasis and to show natural pauses in speech. When there is an occasional end rhyme (calm/palm), the reader's attention becomes as focused as it is in the closing couplets to many of Shakespeare's sonnets. Focusing like that brings Walcott's use of consonance to the foreground. The use of repeated short vowels (corn crop, fort) increases the cadence at which the words proceed. The use of sibilants and some longer vowels ("Crazed by such paradisal calm / the spinal shadow of a palm") slows the telling down.

## Themes

For Walcott, explorers of the Caribbean are fascinating thematic figures. He is deeply impressed by thoughts of the first European men to discover and visit the world to which he belongs: "explorers like Columbus, Walter Raleigh, and James Cook, as well as rebels like Toussaint and Henri-Christophe," wrote Joran Mjoberg in his Nobel biography. "To Walcott, Robinson Crusoe, more than anybody else, is a real archetype, and his long poem, 'Crusoe's Island' (published in the 1965 volume *The Castaway*), contains in addition to a detailed geographic and psychological characterization, simple, lucid lines like the[se]."[2]

# Commentary

Walcott grew up on a small volcanic island, a former colony of both England and France by turns during the last few centuries, one of the Windward Islands in the Lesser Antilles. Instead of the fantasy Daniel Defoe wrote about the castaway Robinson Crusoe, Walcott wrote with fidelity about his own perceptions of life in the islands, far from crowded civilizations.

Islands are by definition isolated from the mainland, and island communities are also separated from the mainland cultures even if there is frequent and regular communication. The poet is describing here the feeling of going mad not only for want of any human company, but specifically for the company of a like mind. It is not hard to see the poet describing his own frustration. If goats, plants, and Friday were not enough company for Crusoe, it is understandable that Walcott would be pining for a like mind among the small population of Saint Lucia. Walcott did find his own metaphorical boat to journey in search of a like mind, and it is worth noting that while he left the island for the wider world, he returns to it each year and calls it home.

Readers can learn the rhythm of Walcott's language, a hybrid between West Indian dialect and literary British dialect, part plain hard work and part wild frustration, by reading this poem aloud; but the poet writes most of his work in standard English. Unlike his contemporary, Kamau Brathwaite, who writes in West Indian dialect, Walcott intends that anyone could read most of his poems in any accent without feeling the poems were written in dialect.

# Codicil

Schizophrenic, wrenched by two styles,
one a hack's hired prose, I earn
me exile. I trudge this sickle, moonlit beach for miles,

tan, burn
to slough off
this live of ocean that's self-love.

To change your language you must change your life.

I cannot right old wrongs.
Waves tire of horizon and return.
Gulls screech with rusty tongues

Above the beached, rotting pirogues,
they were a venomous beaked cloud at Charlotteville.

Once I thought love of country was enough,
now, even if I chose, there is no room at the trough.

I watch the best minds rot like dogs
for scraps of flavour.
I am nearing middle
age, burnt skin
peels from my hand like paper, onion-thin,
like Peer Gynt's riddle.

*At heart there is nothing, not the dread*
*of death. I know too many dead.*
*They're all familiar, all in character,*

*even how they died. On fire,*
*the flesh no longer fears that furnace mouth*
*of earth,*

*that kiln or ashpit of the sun,*
*nor this clouding, unclouding sickle moon*
*withering this beach again like a blank page.*

*All its indifference is a different rage.*

**codicil**—a statement added to a will

**pirogues**—small boats rowed by fishermen

**Charlotteville**—a town on the island of St. Lucia, also called Charlotte, named for Queen Charlotte, the wife of King George III of Britain; she was an enthusiastic supporter of the arts and was rumored to have an African ancestor.

**Peer Gynt's riddle**—the riddle from the play *Peer Gynt* by Henrik Ibsen is: What is it, to be one's self? Peer's answer: "I've always endeavoured to be myself. For the rest, here's my passport, see?" But he is later told by a figure of death that "To be one's self is to deny one's self."

*Excerpt from the essay*

# "The Muse of History"

*(published in 1976)*

*… I accept this archipelago of the Americas, I say to the ancestor who sold me, and to the ancestor who bought me, I have no father, I want no such father, although I can understand you, black ghost, white ghost, when you both whisper "history," for if I attempt to forgive you both I am falling into your idea of history which justifies and explains and expiates, and it is not mine to forgive, my memory cannot summon any filial love, since your features are anonymous and erased and I have no wish and no power to pardon. You were when you acted your roles, your given, historical roles of slave seller and slave buyer, men acting as men, and also you, father in the filth-ridden gut of the slave ship, to you they were also men, your fellowman and tribesman not moved or hovering with hesitation about your common race any longer than my other bastard ancestor hovered with his whip, but to you, inwardly forgiven grandfathers, I, like the more honest of my race, give a strange thanks.*

## Critical Response To Walcott

It is impossible to discuss Walcott and his poetry without acknowledging his mixed racial heritage. Even his Nobel Lectures biography states that "Walcott has been an assiduous traveller to other countries but has always, not least in his efforts to create an indigenous drama, felt himself deeply-rooted in Caribbean society with its cultural fusion of African, Asiatic and European elements."[3] It is the belief of Patrick Bixby that "Walcott's art arises from this schizophrenic situation, from a struggle between two cultural heritages, which he has harnessed to create a unique 'creolized' style."[4]

Another biographer wrote:

> This reconciliation has cost Walcott much but provided him with deep inner peace. But if we think of its universal consequences, this does not mean that there should exist any universal forgiveness for brutality. Thus, Walcott has no forgiveness when he asks in *Omeros* whether he might have broken his pen when he started writing poetry forty years earlier, if he had realized that
> *this century's pastorals were being written*
> *by the chimneys of Dachau, of Auschwitz, of Sachsenhausen.*[5]

## Suggested Further Reading

African writers of great talent but who are almost unknown in English include Ahmadou Kourouma, and the griots and jelis Dimi Mint Abba, Habib Koité, and Mamadou Diabaté. Anne Cameron is a poet and writer whose mixed heritage (British/Canadian First Nations) has brought inspiration and power to her writing. Another writer of mixed Caribbean heritage is Nalo Hopkinson, whose imaginative works have great realism and appeal.

# Leonard Cohen

## (1934–)

On September 21, 1934, Leonard Norman Cohen was born in the Westmount neighborhood of Montreal, Quebec, in Canada. His family were middle-class Jews of Polish-Lithuanian ancestry. As a child, he was told that he was descended from the priestly line of Aaron, as were many other Jewish families with names similar to Cohen. Young Leonard enjoyed a close relationship with his mother, Masha, and his grandfathers, who were both rabbis. His maternal grandfather, Solomon Klinitsky-Klein, was a talmudic scholar and author who would study for hours with young Leonard, discussing the meaning of a single sentence. His paternal grandfather, Lyon Cohen, presided over the synagogue the family attended regularly, and founded the Canadian Jewish Congress in 1919. His father, Nathan Cohen, was an engineer and owner of a clothing concern, and he died when Leonard was only nine, leaving a modest trust fund income that allowed him to pursue an education and literary ambitions.

His uncles were influential in Jewish institutions in Montreal; they wanted him to enter the garment industry. But instead, in a Montreal bookshop at age fifteen, young Leonard found the poetry of Federico García Lorca and had an epiphany, consciously adopting the vision and sensual imagery of Lorca.

Leonard Cohen in concert, 1985

At seventeen, Cohen went to McGill University, where he met poet Irving Layton who became his mentor and lifelong friend. While at McGill, Cohen formed a country and western trio named the Buckskin Boys. His first book of poetry, *Let Us Compare Mythologies*, was published in 1956 by Louis Dudek as the first book in the McGill Poetry Series, while Cohen was still an undergraduate at twenty-two. He then spent a term in law school and a year at Columbia University before dropping out.

*The Spice Box of Earth* (1961), Cohen's second poetry collection, brought him international recognition and a travel grant from the Canada Council for the Arts. Funded by this grant, he traveled throughout Europe, settling on the island of Hydra in Greece with Marianne Jensen and her young son. He applied a strong work ethic to his writing, beginning the production of a substantial body of work.

A successful poet with several published books, Cohen returned to North America in 1967 to become a songwriter. Several singers recorded his works, both before and after he signed with Columbia Records. He has created many albums, all of which have sold better in Europe and Canada than in the United States, though he toured all these places. During the Yom Kippur War in 1973, Cohen toured Israel and performed at army bases. In 1985, Cohen added Poland to his European tour, performing in Warsaw and in Wroclaw's Hala Ludowa, a place where Hitler had addressed crowds of his Nazi followers. For many Poles, Cohen's performances were a political manifestation, part of the Solidarity experience as Poland's trade unions led a popular movement that saw the defeat of the Polish Communist government through free elections. Songs from Cohen albums have been featured in many successful films, from the sound track to the film *McCabe & Mrs. Miller* by Robert Altman, to *Pump Up the Volume, Natural Born Killers,* and *Shrek.*

Cohen married Suzanne Elrod in the 1970s, and they had two children, a son named Adam and a daughter named Lorca. He and Elrod divorced in 1979.

After a tour to promote his latest album, in 1994, Cohen entered the Mount Baldy Zen Center to live in seclusion. He was ordained as a Rinzai Zen Buddhist monk, taking the Dharma name Jikhan, which means silence. Though he left the center in 1999 to create and produce new songs, he has not abandoned his Zen studies. The dark mood of his poetry has brightened in his later years; in interviews, Cohen attributes this to his depression lifting due to the neurological processes of aging. He still applies a strong work ethic to his writing and makes use of the studying skills he learned with his grandfather. For his poem "Closing Time," he composed over a hundred verses, which he edited down to a length and content appropriate for a popular song.

In 2005, Cohen sued his longtime former manager, Kelley Lynch, claiming she had misappropriated the publishing rights to his songs and more than $5 million, emptying his retirement fund. He won the civil suit, but Lynch did not respond to subpoenas. Still working under new management, Cohen made his first public appearance in thirteen years in 2006, at a bookstore in Toronto to promote his newest book of poetry and drawings.

## FACTS

### Turning Down the Prize

In 1968, Cohen declined to accept the Governor General's Award for Poetry, Canada's most prestigious literary prize. He sent a telegram to the master of ceremonies, saying, "Though much in me craves this award, the poems absolutely forbid it." That evening in Ottawa at a party in a hotel suite, Cohen was cornered in the bathroom by Mordecai Richler, a fellow writer and Montreal Jew, who sternly asked why he refused the award. Cohen admitted he did not know. "Any other answer and I would have punched you in the nose," Richler replied.[1]

# Suzanne

*(from the album* Songs of Leonard Cohen, *1967)*

Suzanne takes you down to her place near the river
You can hear the boats go by
You can spend the night beside her
And you know that she's half crazy
But that's why you want to be there
And she feeds you tea and oranges
That come all the way from China
And just when you mean to tell her
That you have no love to give her
Then she gets you on her wavelength
And she lets the river answer
That you've always been her lover.
And you want to travel with her
And you want to travel blind
And you know that she will trust you
For you've touched her perfect body with your mind.

Jesus was a sailor
When he walked upon the water
And he spent a long time watching
From his lonely wooden tower
And when he knew for certain
Only drowning men could see him
He said "All men will be sailors then
Until the sea shall free them."
Ah, but he himself was broken

Long before the sky would open
Forsaken, almost human
He sank beneath your wisdom like a stone.
And you want to travel with him
You want to travel blind
And you think maybe you'll trust him
For he's touched your perfect body with his mind.

Now Suzanne takes your hand
And she leads you to the river
She is wearing rags and feathers
From Salvation Army counters
And the sun pours down like honey
On our lady of the harbour
As she shows you where to look
Among the garbage and the flowers
There are heroes in the seaweed
There are children in the morning
They are leaning out for love
And they will lean that way forever
While Suzanne holds the mirror.
And you want to travel with her
You want to travel blind
And you know that you can trust her
For she's touched your perfect body with her mind.

## Summary and Explication

The speaker tells of visiting Suzanne's home by the river. They are not physically intimate, but he wants to understand this mystic woman. He thinks of Jesus who died to save all people, and he wants to believe in that. He realizes that Suzanne is living in a way that finds art and sustains the people around her, and he wants to do that too.

## Poetic Techniques

In this and other songs, "Cohen does not use a strict rhyming pattern," says Christoph Herold; "instead, he creates a sound structure, or phonological cohesion … by using rhymes, pararhymes, assonances, consonances, inner rhymes and alliterations."[2] Choosing deceptively simple words about seemingly ordinary things, the poet gradually builds a poem that begins a metaphoric journey from home toward salvation.

## Themes

Cohen admits that ever since he could remember, he has been completely obsessed with women. "You have to write about something. Women stand for the objective world for a man," he said in an interview. "They stand for the thing that you're not and that's what you always reach for in a song."[3] In several poems and songs by Cohen, women are regarded as the agents and voice of human civilization, like Shamhat in *Gilgamesh*.

This poem is not a vague beatnik counterculture rant or an adoring hymn praising woman for her beauty and nothing more—it is a tightly controlled poem about the poet recognizing the creative and caring genius in someone else. When she feeds him a modest meal, it is not bread and water but delicacies brought from the Far East. He perceives that Suzanne is not only able to clothe herself out of secondhand stores run by Christian missions, she is able to create art out of rubbish. She is sustaining the heroes and children of her culture by reflecting them in her art and life. Ultimately, she is living a life like that of Christ, caring for people.

# Commentary

This was an early poem in Cohen's second career as a songwriter, and the first time he performed "Suzanne" in public at a benefit concert, he was so insecure that he walked offstage in the middle of it. He did return to complete the song, only at the encouragement of singer Judy Collins, whose acclaimed recording of "Suzanne" had been released a year earlier. The song has been recorded by dozens of artists.

A fan on a music Web site wrote:

> Really, when you listen to the lyrics (or rather poems) of his songs, there is the obvious sexual tension to the words, but more so than that his intelligence and philosophy touches you on a much deeper level than the fact that his appeal to women is incredibly irresistible. A friend of mine remembers him from his early days in Montreal and recalls his almost hypnotic charm on the female of the species; he had women following him everywhere.[4]

When interviewed about this poem at a 2006 conference for Cohen fans in Edmonton, Cohen professed that he was not trying to be allegorical. Suzanne Verdal, wife of sculptor Armand Vaillancourt, *did* take him to her place by the Saint Lawrence River in Montreal. She *did* feed him tea and oranges, and they *were* from China. And they were not intimate; it was only later that he thought about the meeting of their minds. Verdal said in a 1992 CBC radio interview that they met again after a 1970s concert and briefly by accident more than twenty years later, on a street corner in Venice Beach, California, where she was performing modern dance and living in her car. He may not have recognized her.

# Famous Blue Raincoat

*(from the album* Songs of Love and Hate, *1971)*

*It's four in the morning, the end of December*
*I'm writing you now just to see if you're better*
*New York is cold, but I like where I'm living*
*There's music on Clinton Street all through the evening.*

*I hear that you're building your little house deep in the desert*
*You're living for nothing now, I hope you're keeping some kind of record.*

*Yes, and Jane came by with a lock of your hair*
*She said that you gave it to her*
*That night that you planned to go clear*
*Did you ever go clear?*

*Ah, the last time we saw you you looked so much older*
*Your famous blue raincoat was torn at the shoulder*
*You'd been to the station to meet every train*
*And still you came home without Lili Marlene*

*And you treated my woman to a flake of your life*
*And when she came back she was nobody's wife.*
*Well I see you there with the rose in your teeth*
*One more thin gypsy thief*
*Well I see Jane's awake—*

*She sends her regards.*
*And what can I tell you my brother, my killer*
*What can I possibly say?*
*I guess that I miss you, I guess I forgive you*
*I'm glad you stood in my way.*

*If you ever come by here, for Jane or for me*
*Your enemy is sleeping, and his woman is free.*

*Yes, and thanks for the trouble you took from her eyes*
*I thought it was there for good so I never tried.*

*And Jane came by with a lock of your hair*
*She said that you gave it to her*
*That night that you planned to go clear.*

*Sincerely, L. Cohen.*

*Excerpt from*

## Closing Time

*(from the album* The Future, *1992)*

Ah we're drinking and we're dancing
and the band is really happening
and the Johnny Walker wisdom running high
And my very sweet companion
she's the Angel of Compassion
she's rubbing half the world against her thigh.
And every drinker every dancer
lifts a happy face to thank her
the fiddler fiddles something so sublime
all the women tear their blouses off
and the men they dance on the polka-dots
and it's partner found, it's partner lost
and it's hell to pay when the fiddler stops:
it's CLOSING TIME....

I loved you for your beauty
but that doesn't make a fool of me:
you were in it for your beauty too
and I loved you for your body
there's a voice that sounds like God to me
declaring, declaring, declaring that your body's
really you.
And I loved you when our love was blessed
and I love you now there's nothing left
but sorrow and a sense of overtime
And I missed you since the place got wrecked
and I just don't care what happens next
looks like freedom but it feels like death
it's something in between, I guess
it's CLOSING TIME....

## Critical Response To Leonard Cohen

"It's hard to think of another artist who cares so little for or about pop music yet who has changed it, and influenced its practitioners, so profoundly as Leonard Cohen,"[5] wrote music critic Nick Dedina. There are more than twelve hundred released versions of Cohen's songs. His poetry is acclaimed as well. On the publication of *Beautiful Losers,* Cohen's fifth book, the *Boston Globe* declared, "James Joyce is not dead. He is living in Montreal under the name of Cohen."[6]

While Sin-leqi-unninni was one of a handful of composers in Babylon, and Dante was one of a few dozens of European poets in his lifetime, Cohen is only one of hundreds of professional songwriters and thousands of amateurs composing in English at the beginning of the twenty-first century. He is among the best of the internationally recognized poets born overseas from their ancestors' places of origin; these foreign-born offspring of immigrant parents (called *nisei* in Japanese, and *illahie* in Chinook jargon) bring an awareness of their ancestral roots to the mosaic cultures in which they are educated and working. Cohen is also recognized as being among the best of the poets composing in English, in colonial countries, and former British colonies, such as Canada.

"Only in Canada could somebody with a voice like mine win 'Vocalist of the Year,' said Cohen, when he was awarded the Juno for his gravelly bass-baritone that rasps with age.[7] Among his many awards, Cohen has been inducted into the Rock and Roll Hall of Fame, the Canadian Songwriters Hall of Fame, and the Canadian Music Hall of Fame. He is a Companion of the Order of Canada, that nation's highest honor for civilians.

## Suggested Further Reading

Look to Farron, Bob Dylan, and Tom Waits for singers and lyricists in English with some similar strengths. For nonmusical verses, look to the poetry of P. K. Page, Milton Acorn, and New Guinean poets writing in pidgin.

## Introduction

1. Marshall McLuhan, *Understanding Media: The Extensions of Man*, quoted by Judith Fitzgerald in "The Dancer and His Cain," n.d., <http://www.judithfitzgerald.ca/famousblueraincoat.html> (March 5, 2008).
2. Ursula Le Guin, *Always Coming Home* (Los Angeles, Calif.: University of California Press, 2000).

## Chapter 1. Sin-leqi-unninni, the Gilgamesh poet

1. Stephen Mitchell, "Introduction," *Gilgamesh: A New English Version* (New York: Free Press, 2004), p. 1.
2. Derrek Hines, "Introduction," *Gilgamesh* (Toronto, Ontario: Random House, 2002), p. ix.
3. Ibid., p. x.
4. Arthur A. Brown, "Storytelling, the Meaning of Life, and the Epic of Gilgamesh," *Exploring Ancient World Cultures Web site*, 1996, <http://eawc.evansville.edu/essays/brown.htm> (December 28, 2007).
5. George Smith, *The Chaldean Account of Genesis* (London, UK: Samson Low, Marston, Searle and Rivington, 1876), pp. 4–5.
6. Rainer Maria Rilke, "Letter to Helene von Nostiz, New Year's Eve, 1916," *Briefwechsel mit Helene von Nostitz* (Germany: Insel Verlag, 1976), p. 99.
7. Rainer Maria Rilke, "Letter to Katharina Kippenberg, December 11, 1916," *Briefwechsel: Rainer Maria Rilke und Katharina Kippenberg* (Germany: Insel Verlag, 1954), p. 191.
8. Mitchell, p. 2.
9. Hines, p. 3.

## Chapter 2. Vyasa, the Mahabharata poet

1. John Bruno Hare, Excerpt from "Book One, Adi Parva, Section One," *The Mahabharata. Internet Sacred Text Archive Web site*, n.d., <http://www.sacred-texts.com/hin/maha/index.htm> (January 12, 2008).
2. James L. Fitzgerald, "The Great Epic of India," *The Mahabharata Web site*, 1999, <http://web.utk.edu/~jftzgrld/MBh1Home.html> (January 19, 2008).

## Chapter 3.  Homer

1. Carlos Parada, "Briseis," *Greek Mythology Link Web site,* 1997–2007, <http://homepage.
   mac.com/cparada/GML/Briseis.html> (February 7, 2008).
2. "The Greek Poet Homer," *Mythography: Exploring Greek, Roman, and Celtic Mythology
   and Art, Loggia.com,* 1997–2006, <http://www.loggia.com/myth/homer.html> (February
   7, 2008).

## Chapter 4. Du Fu

1. Ian P. McGreal, ed., "The Poetry of Du Fu," *Great Literature of the Eastern World* (New
   York: HarperCollins, 1996), p. 81.
2. Eva Shan Chou, "The Legacy of Tu Fu," *Reconsidering Tu Fu: Literary Greatness and
   Cultural Context* (Cambridge: Cambridge University Press, 1995), p. 2.
3. Ibid., p. 1.

## Chapter 5. Omar Khayyam

1. Reynard Alleyne Nicholson, "Introduction," *Rubaiyat of Omar Khayyam* (New York:
   Smithmark Publishers Inc., 1998), p. 16.
2. Ibid., "Notes," p. 137.
3. "Omar Khayyam," *The Columbia Electronic Encyclopedia Web site*, 2007 <http://www.
   infoplease.com/ce6/people/A0836626.html> (January 13, 2008).
4. Genesis 3:19, "The Fall of Man," *Byblos.com Web site,* <http://bible.cc/genesis/3-19.htm>
   (February 26, 2008).
5. Nicholson, p. 14.
6. Shariar Shahriari, *Rubaiyat of Omar Khayyam Web site,* 1998–2003, <http://www.
   okonlife.com/poems> (January 21, 2008).

## Chapter 6. Rumi

1. Jean Claude Carriere, "Introduction," in *Love: The Joy That Wounds,* Mahin and Nahal
   Tajadad and Elfreda Powell, trans. (London: Souvenir Press, 2005), p. 7.
2. Rumi, "Melvana—Rumi Profile, Rumi Quotes," *Quote Monk Web site,* n.d., <http://
   www.quotemonk.com/authors/rumi-mevlana/index.htm> (February 17, 2008).
3. Maryam Mafi and Azima Melita Kolin, trans., *Rumi: Hidden Music,* (London: Thorsons/
   HarperCollins, 2001), p. viii.
4. Carriere, p. 8.
5. Rumi, "Melvana—Rumi Profile, Rumi Biography," *Quote Monk Web site*, n.d., <http://
   www.quotemonk.com/authors/rumi-mevlana/index.htm> (February 17, 2008).

## Chapter 7. Dante

1. The Digital Dante Project, *The Concise Columbia Encyclopedia Web site,* Columbia
   University Press, 1991, <http://dante.ilt.columbia.edu/new/> (December 20, 2007).
2. Russell McNeil, *A Short History of Hell,* 2005, <http://www.malaspina.org/dantea.htm>
   (February 2, 2008).
3. Ibid.

4. Nick Kyriazes, "Dante, Lust, and Modern 'Sensibility,'" *Dante's Inferno Web site,* n.d., <http://personal.monm.edu/nkyriaze/inferno.htm> (March 4, 2008).

## Chapter 8. Bashō

1. Sam Hamill, "Translator's Introduction," *The Sound of Water,* November 2006, <http://www.shambhala.com/html/catalog/items/isbn/978-1-57062-019-5. cfm?selectedText=EXCERPT_CHAPTER> (December 9, 2009).
2. "Basho, Matsuo," *New World Encyclopedia,* n.d., <http://www.newworldencyclopedia. org/entry/Matsuo_/basho> (August 4, 2009).
3. Eri F. Yasuhara, "Review," *One Hundred Frogs: From Rengu to Haiku in English by Hiroaki Sato* (Tokyo and New York: John Weatherhill, 1983), Monumenta Nipponica, vol. 38, no. 4 (Winter, 1983), pp. 440–442.
4. Soji, "Bashō's Hut," *The Haiku Poets Hut Web site,* 1996–2008, <http://www. haikupoetshut.com/Bashōndx-1024.html> (February 3, 2008).
5. Sam Hamill, "Translator's Introduction," *The Sound of Water,* November 2006, <http://www.shambhala.com/html/catalog/items/isbn/978-1-57062-019-5. cfm?selectedText=EXCERPT_CHAPTER> (December 9, 2009).

## Chapter 9. Taras Shevchenko

1. "Shevchenko's Art," *Taras Shevchenko Museum Web site,* 2007, <http://www.infoukes. com/shevchenkomuseum/poetry> (January 18, 2008).
2. "Biography of Taras Shevchenko," *Taras Shevchenko Museum Web site,* 2007, <http:// www.infoukes.com/shevchenkomuseum/poetry> (January 18, 2008).

## Chapter 10. Rabindranath Tagore

1. Prima Sounds Foundation, "Rabindranath Tagore Classes," *School of Wisdom Web site,* n.d., <http://www.schoolofwisdom.com/tagore-bio.html> (January 20, 2008).
2. Horst Frenz, Nobel Lectures, Literature 1901–1967 (Amsterdam, N. Dak.: Elsevier Publishing, 1969), *Nobel Prize Web site,* <http://nobelprize.org/nobel_prizes/literature/ laureates/1913/tagore-bio.html> (January 23, 2008).

## Chapter 11. Anna Akhmatova

1. Sir Isaiah Berlin, "Conversations with Akhmatova and Pasternak," *The Proper Study of Mankind* (New York: Farrar, Straus & Giroux, 1998).
2. Petri Luikkonen, "Anna Akhmatova," *Books and Writers Web site,* 2002, <http://www. kirjasto.sci.fi/aakhma.htm> (December 15, 2008).
3. Clive James, "Anna Akhmatova: Assessing the Russian poet and femme fatale," *Slate Web site,* February 5, 2007, <http://www.slate.com/id/2159089> (December 15, 2007).

## Chapter 12. Federico García Lorca

1. Francisco Soto, "Garcia Lorca, Federico," *GLBTQ.com Literature,* Chicago, Ill.: New England Publishing Associates, 2002, <http://www.glbtq.com/literature/garcialorca_f. html> (June 10, 2009).

2. Robert Pring-Mill, "Federico García Lorca," Alan Bullock, R. B. Woodings, and John Cumming, eds., *Fontana Biographical Companion to Modern Thought,* 1983, <http://www.boppin.com/lorca> (December 18, 2007).

## Chapter 13. Pablo Neruda

1. Pablo Neruda, "Pablo Neruda," *Famous Poets and Poems.com Web site,* n.d., <http://famouspoetsandpoems.com/poets/pablo_neruda> (January 10, 2008).
2. Smith and Lewalski, "William Shakespeare," M. H. Abrams et al., eds., *The Norton Anthology of English Literature,* 5th ed., vol. 1. (Markham, Ontario: Penguin Books, Canada, 1962), p. 867.
3. Katharena Eiermann,. "Pablo Neruda," *Aspirennies.com Web site,* 1997–2008, <http://www.aspirennies.com/private/SiteBody/Romance/Poetry/Neruda/pneruda.shtml> (January 10, 2008).
4. Neruda.

## Chapter 14. Derek Walcott

1. Joran Mjoberg, "A Single, Homeless, Circling Satellite: Derek Walcott, 1992 Nobel Literature Laureate," June 26, 2001, *The Official Web Site of the Nobel Foundation,* <http://nobelprize.org/nobel_prizes/literature/articles/mjoberg/index.html> (January 6, 2008).
2. Ibid.
3. Sture Allén, ed., "Derek Walton biography," *Nobel Lectures, Literature 1991–1995* (Singapore: World Scientific Publishing Co., 1997).
4. Patrick Bixby, "Derek Walcott," *Postcolonial Studies at Emory,* 2000, <http://www.english.emory.edu/Bahri/Walcott.html> (January 10, 2008).
5. Mjoberg.

## Chapter 15. Leonard Cohen

1. Sheldon Teitelbaun, "Leonard Cohen, Pain Free," *Los Angeles Times,* April 5, 1992.
2. Christoph Herold, "Famous Blue Raincoat: an approach to an integrated analysis of a song," *Heroldmusic Web site,* n.d., <http://www.heroldmusic.com/assets/Famous_Blue_Raincoat__English.pdf> (March 3, 2008).
3. Leonard Cohen, interviewed on Assignment, *CBC Radio,* June 16, 1961, *CBC Web site,* February 28, 2008, <http://archives.cbc.ca/IDC-1-68-93-441/arts_entertainment/leonard_cohen/clip2> (March 3, 2008).
4. Geri [last name withheld], "Famous Blue Raincoat by Leonard Cohen," *Songfacts Web site,* n.d., <http://www.songfacts.com/detail.php?id=2580> (March 3, 2008).
5. Nick Dedina, "Leonard Cohen," *Rhapsody Web site,* n.d., <http://www.rhapsody.com/leonardcohen#> (February 15, 2008).
6. Larry Sloman, "A Short Biography of Leonard Cohen," *The Leonard Cohen Files Web site,* n.d., <http://www.leonardcohenfiles.com/yourman.html> (March 3, 2008).
7. Leonard Cohen, interviewed on *Friday Night with Ralph Benmergui,* CBC-TV, February 12, 1993.

# GLOSSARY

**alliteration**—The repetition of an initial consonant sound.

**assonance**—The repetition of a vowel sound.

**commedia**—An Italian work of verse representing a story with varied content and style leading to a happy ending, as opposed to a tragedy, which ends badly.

**consonance**—Harmony or agreement of sounds in words.

**couplet**—A pair of lines with end rhyme.

**doggerel**—Casual verse, usually considered clumsy and with little artistic merit.

**foot**—The basic unit of verse meter in poetry; a unit of syllables within a line, with one stressed syllable and three, two, one, or no unstressed syllables.

**glosa**—A Spanish verse form in tribute to four lines by another poet. A glosa has four stanzas of ten lines, each stanza beginning with one of the lines of the other poet's verse.

**griot**—A West African poet and singer of traditional stories and family histories.

**imagery**—The vivid depiction of a sensory image.

**jeli**—A traditional West African poet and entertainer.

**lushi**—A form of Chinese poetry; an octave, or eight-line verse.

**metaphor**—A statement describing a particular quality of one thing by saying that it is another.

**meter**—The measure of systematically arranged rhythm in poetry, in units of syllables within a line.

**pararhyme**—The use of words that have some similar sounds but do not rhyme precisely.

**pseudonym**—A pen name used by an author instead of his or her legal name, sometimes a beloved nickname, sometimes for anonymity or to keep a family name from being associated with published works.

**rhyme**—The repetition of similar sounds; lines of poetry may rhyme within the line or more usually at its end with another line; one-syllable rhyme (red/dead) is called male rhyme, two-or-more-syllable rhyme (pilaster/alabaster) is called female rhyme.

**ruba'i**—A form of Farsi poetry; a quatrain, or four-line verse.

**samizdat (SAH-meez-dot)**—Amateur publications created and circulated unofficially, when government approval is needed for any published work; often samizdat has a political component, either by design or simply by not meeting government approval.

**scop**—A traditional Anglo-Saxon poet and performer.

**simile**—A statement describing a particular quality of a thing by saying that it is like something else.

**skald**—A traditional Scandinavian poet.

**sonnet**—A poem with fourteen lines of iambic pentameter verse, with a variety of rhyme patterns, based on an Italian form ("little song") made popular by Petrarch.

**stanza**—A verse or set of lines grouped together and set apart from the rest of the poem, like a paragraph in prose writing.

**stock epithet**—A standard phrase repeatedly used in epic poetry to name and describe a character, such as "the wily Odysseus" or "fair-cheeked Briseis," or to describe a common event, such as "gashed with the mangling bronze"; especially the standard phrases used by Homer in the *Iliad* and the *Odyssey*.

**symbol**—Something that stands for a larger idea.

# Further Reading

## Books

Bloom, Harold. *The Best Poems of the English Language: From Chaucer Through Robert Frost.* New York: HarperCollins, 2004.

McGreal, Ian P., ed. *Great Literature of the Eastern World.* New York: HarperCollins, 1996.

Parisi, Joseph, and Stephen Young, eds. *The Poetry Anthology.* Chicago: Ivan R. Dee, 2004.

Polonsky, Marc. *The Poetry Reader's Toolkit: A Guide to Reading and Understanding Poetry.* Lincolnwood, Ill.: NTC Publishing Group, 1998.

Washington, Peter, ed. *Haiku.* New York: Alfred A. Knopf, 2003.

## Internet Addresses

Archive of Classic Poems
<http://www.everypoet.com/archive/>

The Poetry Archive
<http://www.poetryarchive.org>

Poetry Foundation
<http://www.poetryfoundation.org>

INDEX